Withdrawn

METH

BY SUE BRADFORD EDWARDS

CONTENT CONSULTANT

SOWMYA V. YELAMANCHILI, PHD

ASSISTANT PROFESSOR, DEPARTMENT OF
PHARMACOLOGY AND EXPERIMENTAL NEUROSCIENCE
UNIVERSITY OF NEBRASKA MEDICAL CENTER

Essential Library

An Imprint of Abdo Publishing | abdopublishing.com

ABDOPUBLISHING.COM

Published by Abdo Publishing, a division of ABDO, PO Box 398166, Minneapolis, Minnesota 55439.
Copyright © 2019 by Abdo Consulting Group, Inc. International copyrights reserved in all countries.
No part of this book may be reproduced in any form without written permission from the publisher.
Essential Library™ is a trademark and logo of Abdo Publishing.

Printed in the United States of America, North Mankato, Minnesota
042018
092018

THIS BOOK CONTAINS
RECYCLED MATERIALS

Cover Photo: J. T. Sorrell/iStockphoto
Interior Photos: Liz Wilkinson/Joliet News-Herald/AP Images, 4–5; Denny Simmons/The Evansville
Courier & Press/AP Images, 7; Shawn Patrick Ouellette/Portland Press Herald/Getty Images, 10–11;
iStockphoto, 14–15; B. Christopher/Alamy, 20–21; Jeanne Miller Wood/Washington Missourian/
AP Images, 22; Ben Benton/Daily Post-Athenian/AP Images, 25; Science Source, 27; Shutterstock
Images, 30 (top), 30 (middle), 30 (bottom), 42, 49; Bob Chamberlin/Los Angeles Times/Getty Images,
34; Multnomah County Sheriff's Office/Barcroft Media/Getty Images, 37; James A. Finley/AP Images,
39; Tim Sloan/AFP/Getty Images, 44–45; Courtesy of Dr. Douglas Damm/The News & Observer/
AP Images, 47; Mark Boster/Los Angeles Times/Getty Images, 50–51; Jonathan Torgovnik/Getty
Images News/Getty Images, 54; Gary Friedman/Los Angeles Times/Getty Images, 60; Peter Morgan/
AP Images, 63; Red Line Editorial, 66; John Cross/The Mankato Free Press/AP Images, 68–69; Jeff
Roberson/AP Images, 72–73, 84–85; Brendan Smialowski/Getty Images News/Getty Images, 77;
Kelley McCall/AP Images, 79; C. H. Pete Copelane/The Plain Dealer/AP Images, 82; Bruno Gonzalez/
AP Images, 88–89; Jim Salter/AP Images, 90; AP Images, 94; William Campbell/Corbis News/Getty
Images, 98–99

Editor: Rebecca Rowell
Series Designer: Laura Polzin

Library of Congress Control Number: 2017961354

Publisher's Cataloging-in-Publication Data

Names: Edwards, Sue Bradford, author.
Title: Meth / by Sue Bradford Edwards.
Description: Minneapolis, Minnesota : Abdo Publishing, 2019. | Series: Drugs in real life | Includes
online resources and index.
Identifiers: ISBN 9781532114182 (lib.bdg.) | ISBN 9781532154010 (ebook)
Subjects: LCSH: Methamphetamine--Juvenile literature. | Recreational drug use--Juvenile literature.
| Drug control--United States--Juvenile literature. | Drug addiction--Juvenile literature.
Classification: DDC 362.299--dc23

CONTENTS

CHAPTER ONE
FIGHTING FIRE
4

CHAPTER TWO
ABOUT METH
14

CHAPTER THREE
METH AND THE BRAIN
26

CHAPTER FOUR
OTHER PHYSICAL EFFECTS
36

CHAPTER FIVE
PERSONAL EFFECTS
50

CHAPTER SIX
QUITTING METH
62

CHAPTER SEVEN
LEGAL CONSEQUENCES
72

CHAPTER EIGHT
THE CURRENT SITUATION
84

ESSENTIAL FACTS   100   SOURCE NOTES   106

GLOSSARY   102   INDEX   110

ADDITIONAL RESOURCES   104   ABOUT THE AUTHOR   112

FIGHTING FIRE

At three o'clock on the morning of January 9, 2017, emergency operators in Lake Geneva, Wisconsin, received a call. Smoke was coming from a room at the Cove of Lake Geneva, a hotel. The city's police and fire departments responded.

Police officers at the scene immediately noticed something about the smoke. It was not cigarette smoke or ordinary smoke from a building fire. This smoke was pungent, or sharp, and tasted sour. Every breath the officers took burned their throats. Still, they made their way into the hotel room. There, they found a confused man with most of his facial hair burned off.

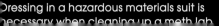

Dressing in a hazardous materials suit is necessary when cleaning up a meth lab.

After firefighters put out the blaze, police officers investigated the room. One firefighter noticed blood and burned clothing on the carpet. Another firefighter entered the bathroom and found charred debris and burn marks on the walls. Something in the bathroom had exploded.

The emergency personnel on the scene found ingredients and equipment used to cook, or make, methamphetamine. This illegal drug is commonly known as meth. The emergency responders found Sudafed tablets, batteries, drain cleaner, cold packs, camping fuel, a bottle, and rubber tubing. Outside the room, lying in the snow, one investigator found a sunglasses case containing two pipes used to smoke meth.

METH'S MANY NAMES

Methamphetamine has many nicknames other than meth. It is also known as chalk, chicken feed, cinnamon, cotton candy, crank, crystal, dunk, getgo, go fast, go-go juice, ice, no doze, redneck cocaine, rocket fuel, speed, tick tick, tina, tweek, uppers, and white cross. Some names, such as ice and cinnamon, play off the appearance of the drug. Others, such as go-go juice and no doze, refer to its stimulant effect on the user.

Lake Geneva's 911 operators received another emergency call at approximately the same time as the call about the fire. Dan Novotny, the chief security officer at a neighboring hotel, was on duty. He heard a woman calling for help in the parking garage. He found Melissa Kuen. "She was burned really bad from head to toe. Her clothes were burned off," said Novotny.[1] She was wearing only a winter coat. Novotny knew nothing about the fire next door. But he knew this woman needed help, so he called 911.

Kuen told police officers she had been burned when someone lit a cigarette while she was helping a friend put gas in a car. Officers quickly realized she was part of the meth accident at the Cove. Kuen was taken to the hospital, where medical staff admitted her and treated her wounds.

Back at the Cove, police officers arrested Patrick McBean, the man in the hotel room. They charged him with possessing meth paraphernalia. On October 25, 2017, McBean pleaded guilty to possessing meth waste. He entered this plea so authorities would drop other charges, including drug trafficking. He was expected

Throughout the United States, firefighters and other emergency workers face the hazards of methamphetamine labs, including explosions and fires.

to go to prison for at least two years before being eligible
for parole.

THE METH EPIDEMIC

Meth is a powerful and highly addictive stimulant. As a stimulant,
it increases alertness and mental and physical activity. Meth is
available in different forms. A person can swallow it as a pill or
heat it in crystal form and inhale the resulting fumes. Meth can
also be dissolved and injected directly into a vein. At one time,
meth was found primarily in poor, rural areas. Today, meth is
common in urban areas. Although the price varies from city to
city, in 2016, a single dose of meth, which weighs 0.009 ounces
(255 mg), costs approximately $25.[2]

Meth causes a rush that is followed by a long-lasting high.
The effects of using meth can vary depending on how it is taken.
When injected or taken by mouth, the effects can last six to eight
hours. When smoked or snorted, they last up to 12 hours.[3]

But meth causes more than the high that users seek. The
drug also causes unpleasant physical effects. Meth makes the
heart beat dangerously fast, increases body temperature, and
results in convulsions.

Even with these negative effects, the number of people in
the United States using meth has grown. In 2010, an estimated
3 percent of the US population used the illegal drug. By 2015,
the figure was 4 percent. More than 300 million people live

in the United States, so each percentage point equals millions of people.[4]

Other meth-related numbers have also increased. In 2014, approximately 3,700 people in the United States died as a result of overdosing on meth. In 2015, that number was 4,900, an increase of 30 percent in a single year.[5] By 2016, the number of deaths from meth overdose had risen to 7,663.[6] That was an increase of more than 56 percent in one year.[7] Not everyone who overdoses dies. But those who survive may face lifelong issues. They may never recover from the physical damage of abusing the drug.

TRACKING METH DEATHS

The Centers for Disease Control and Prevention is the US government agency responsible for public health issues. One of its centers is the National Center for Health Statistics (NCHS). Among the many statistics the center tracks is the number of deaths per year due to meth overdoses. The NCHS also tracks overdoses from other common drugs, including cocaine and heroin.

A DANGEROUS ADDICTION

Meth users are not the only people endangered by the drug. McBean's actions at the Cove affected many people. Kuen was seriously injured and faced the same criminal charges as McBean. In addition, one firefighter, four police officers, and one security guard were treated for smoke inhalation. These eight people had been affected by one batch of meth gone bad.

Law enforcement personnel investigating a possible meth lab in Maine take precautions that include wearing protective gear to guard against possible contamination.

Law enforcement officers in particular face the danger of exposure to meth. They investigate when someone overdoses or starts a fire while cooking meth. They also search for evidence of someone possessing the drug. Police officer Kevin Phillips was at the scene of an overdose in Harford County, Maryland. The victim said drugs were in a nightstand. Philips opened the drawer and felt the effects of meth exposure almost instantaneously. His face felt burning hot, and he started to sweat. His heart rate and blood pressure increased. He and his coworkers in the sheriff's department now wear gloves and masks anytime they might

encounter meth. The sheriff warns his staff that getting the drug on their skin can be almost as dangerous as inhaling it.

But the risk does not end with drug users and emergency workers. When meth is manufactured in a hotel room or a house, the drug and the chemicals used to make it contaminate the building. Anyone who lives or stays in the building can be exposed to the drug. Effective cleanup takes a long time and costs a lot of money.

Following the fire in the Cove, hotel management worked with several remediation companies. These businesses are

OFFICER RISK

Insufficient information has been collected regarding the long-term health effects of meth exposure on emergency personnel who regularly come into contact with the drug, its ingredients, or its waste. The American Detoxification Project (ADP) is trying to change this with its Utah Meth Cops Project. From 2007 to 2010, 69 officers who had been exposed to meth or related chemicals enrolled in this program after suffering from a wide range of symptoms and long-term health problems. For more than 75 percent of participants, issues included fatigue, headaches, insomnia, memory loss, and personality changes.[10] ADP personnel found that the officers all had higher levels of pain and fatigue and significantly more health problems than the general population. ADP thinks these officers developed these symptoms because they were exposed to meth, meth ingredients, and meth waste. Officers are exposed to these harmful chemicals when collecting samples at crime scenes, transporting evidence, and using vehicles that have been contaminated by meth.

experts in cleaning spaces that have been used to prepare drugs. The Cove spent $100,000 to clean and repair the room damaged by the meth explosion in January 2017, but the room still was not ready for guests to use.[8] The hotel decided to replace some things a remediation company said should be cleaned. "They wanted us to decontaminate the original toaster and keep it," Cove general manager Dick Schwalbenberg said. "How can you get contaminants out of a toaster?"[9]

Meth has other effects as well. It also takes a personal toll on people. Users affect those around them, including spouses, children, other family members, and friends.

Despite the severe effects meth has on users and their communities, more people in the

United States are becoming addicted to the drug. Because of this, the US government passed laws to try to curb meth production and use. Such legislation has not helped. The number of meth users continues to rise. Meth is no longer used primarily by poverty-stricken people living in rural areas, which was its initial user base. Now, meth is used by people living in cities and suburbs, often in areas that are also experiencing problems with heroin abuse. Understanding the problems associated with meth begins with understanding what meth is and where it comes from.

Twenty-seven US states require real estate agents to tell buyers a home was contaminated by meth.[11]

CLEANING UP

Alliance Environmental Group, which has offices in California and Arizona, cleans up crime scenes, hoarding environments, and drug houses. The company has cleaned up buildings where meth, heroin, and the painkiller fentanyl have seeped into walls, carpets, and concrete and polluted heating and air-conditioning systems. Alliance receives approximately ten requests for drug-related cleanups per month. Sometimes, the company receives a call from a new homeowner who does not know what is wrong. In one house, the homeowner's children had become sick. Alliance took various samples and found meth. "It's actually more common than you think," said Alliance project manager Robert McKeever.[12]

CHAPTER TWO

ABOUT METH

Meth comes in many forms, which can make it difficult to recognize. Meth can be a tablet, rock, crystal, or powder that can be dissolved in liquid. The crystal form is often called crystal meth and looks like shards of glass.

Meth is odorless and tastes slightly bitter. Meth can be a variety of colors. Pure meth is clear or white. Pure meth is also chemically uniform. This allows it to crystallize, giving it a crystalline structure that reflects all wavelengths of visible light. This reflective ability is what makes it look white or clear. Sometimes, drug dealers dye meth blue. This blue meth is chemically the same as white or clear meth. Meth can also be brown,

Meth's many forms include crystalline.

▶

14

yellow-gray, orange, or pink, taking these colors from impurities or colorings in the ingredients that go into making the drug.

THE APPEAL

Meth appeals to users because it is a stimulant. Stimulants raise activity levels in the body. They wake up people and make them more alert. Caffeine—found in drinks such as coffee, tea, and some soft drinks—is also a stimulant.

Meth is part of a group of stimulants that includes amphetamines and ephedra. The first of these stimulants to be widely used was ephedra, a shrub used in traditional Chinese medicine for more than 5,000 years. Ephedra eases breathing by opening constricted bronchial tubes in the chest. In 1885, Japanese chemist Nagai Nagayoshi, studying in Germany, identified ephedrine, the chemical stimulant in ephedra. While ephedra can be useful, it can also raise blood pressure and irritate the stomach, among other side effects. Because of these negative effects, people

EPHEDRA TODAY

In the United States today, ephedra is often known as ma huang, which is Chinese for "hemp yellow."[1] The name describes the Chinese shrub that is the source of ephedrine. Unlike meth, which is illegal throughout the United States, ephedra is sold legally in some states. The US Food and Drug Administration warns that long-term use of ephedra can damage the central nervous system or heart. Sports organizations have listed the drug as a banned substance, even if an athlete lives in an area where it can be purchased legally.

looked for a chemical substitute that would create the positive effects and not the negative ones.

In 1887, scientists in Germany developed the chemical stimulant amphetamine. They had no specific use for the drug, and it was difficult to make. But in 1919, Japanese chemist Akira Ogata found an easier way to make amphetamine. Using phosphorus and iodine, he produced a crystallized form of the drug. It was the first crystal meth. Researchers investigated various uses for this powerful stimulant, testing its ability to treat a variety of ailments, including congestion and depression. During the 1930s, amphetamine was sold as Benzedrine. This over-the-counter drug, taken using an inhaler like those used for today's asthma medications, was used to treat nasal congestion in people with asthma, hay fever, and head colds.

STIMULANTS GO TO WAR

During World War II (1939–1945), the use of both amphetamines and methamphetamines became more common. German soldiers received meth to boost their morale and keep them alert. Japanese pilots were injected with methamphetamines before going on suicidal missions, flying bomb-loaded planes into US ships.

Militaries were not the only markets for stimulants. During the 1950s, methedrine was sold over the counter in the United States. This form of meth was popular among college students who wanted to stay up late to study, truckers who wanted to be alert while driving long hours and at night, and athletes who were looking for a competitive edge.

Throughout the 1960s, everyday people bought both methamphetamines and amphetamines to lose weight, cope with mild depression, and be more alert. In the 1980s, the United States regulated ephedrine, the principal ingredient in meth at that time. Meth use dropped off until the people who cooked the drug developed a new formula using a different stimulant called pseudoephedrine. With this new formula, meth labs spread throughout the country.

COOKING METH

Many drugs, including marijuana, heroin, and cocaine, come from plants. People grow and harvest the plants, then use various techniques to dry the plant or extract and purify the drug.

THE METH MYTH

Many people believe that if a person uses meth one time, he instantly becomes an addict. This is not true. After using meth once, the person might really want to use again. He might think about it, but he does not yet have the overwhelming drive to do whatever it takes to get more. When this happens, and meth is all the person cares about, when it has taken over his or her life, then the person has an addiction. One 2015 study found that women who had abused meth, amphetamines, or cocaine showed a reduction in the amount of gray matter compared with male stimulant users and men and women who did not use stimulants. Gray matter is the brain tissue that controls behavior, motion, and thought.

Meth is different. It is a combination of chemical ingredients. The base ingredient in most meth is either ephedrine or the pseudoephedrine found in many cold and allergy medications. A meth cook starts with these medications in pill form. Because the pills have ingredients other than pseudoephedrine, they need to be purified and sometimes concentrated. This is where many of the other components of cooking meth come into play.

Each component plays a critical role in the chemical process. Some are solvents that dissolve other components. The solvents used to make meth include acetone, found in nail polish remover; ethyl alcohol, the alcohol in liquor; white gas, the fuel found in camp stoves; and Freon, which is used in air conditioners and refrigerators.

Hydriodic acid is one of the most essential components for cooking meth. Used by oil refineries to test crude oil for sulfur, it acts as a reducing agent. It breaks down the pseudoephedrine molecules, which then recombine as meth.

Other components extract the meth from the mixture. One method uses anhydrous ammonia, which is a chemical fertilizer, and lithium, which comes from batteries. Another method uses red iodine, which is normally used to treat yeast infections on horse hooves.

A final component is red phosphorous, which is found in matchsticks and road flares. It acts as a catalyst, or something that causes a chemical reaction to happen.

Meth's ingredients include common household items.

DANGEROUS COMPONENTS

All the components needed to cook meth are dangerous.
Pseudoephedrine can have serious side effects. Anyone who
ingests more than 0.008 ounces (240 mg) of pseudoephedrine
may experience high blood pressure, an irregular heartbeat,
anxiety, and vomiting. Doses larger than 0.02 ounces (600 mg)
can cause seizures and kidney failure.[2]

Many components are flammable. These include the solvents acetone, ethyl alcohol, and white gas. Anhydrous ammonia is also highly flammable. Unlike the solvents, which need an open flame to ignite, lithium can be flammable when it contacts water. Red phosphorous is explosive under friction.

Other meth components are irritants, damaging various parts of the body. Freon, one of the solvents, can damage the lungs if inhaled or the throat and stomach if swallowed.

The fumes of the reducing agent hydriodic acid irritate the eyes, skin, and respiratory system. Swallowing the acid can be fatal. Gases released when red phosphorous burns irritate the eyes, nose, throat, and lungs. Anhydrous ammonia damages the eyes or other mucous membranes, such as those found in the nose, throat, and lungs. And iodine crystals and red phosphorous are toxic and corrosive, burning the eyes, nose, and skin.

RURAL CRISIS

When meth cooks developed a formula using pseudoephedrine, the number of meth labs in rural areas increased, especially in the Midwest. That is because a key ingredient in this new formula

Michael Murphy, a former meth user, lost sight in both eyes and hearing in one ear when a tank of anhydrous ammonia blew up in his face.

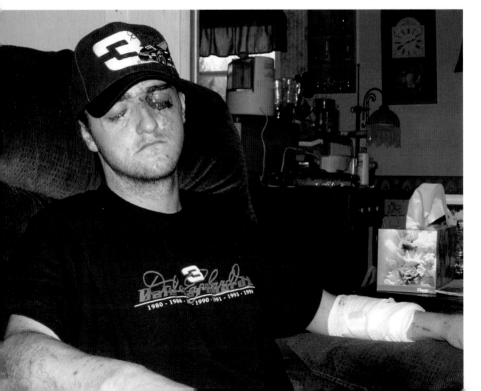

was anhydrous ammonia, a fertilizer kept by farmers in their fields. Farmers and chemical distributors alike learned to look for signs that meth cooks had tapped a tank.

In 2003, law enforcement reported 17,400 meth labs and dump sites to the US Drug Enforcement Agency.[5]

Cooking meth using anhydrous ammonia requires a full laboratory with containers of chemicals and large numbers of pills. Mixtures bubble over open flames. The incredibly bad smell given off by the chemical process is another reason to cook meth in isolated, rural areas. The less dense population decreases the likelihood of being detected.

Fires often broke out in these rural labs. "It was usually on a stove in a back room or garage and people would just run," said Mark Woodward, spokesman for the Oklahoma Bureau of Narcotics and Dangerous Drugs Control.[3] Even if no one is injured, the fire has to be put out, and this requires calling in emergency personnel. First responders are exposed to the dangerous chemicals.

Once firefighters extinguish the flames, the problem becomes the chemical waste that remains. Processing a single pound of meth creates five pounds (2 kg) of toxic waste.[4] Both indoor and outdoor areas become contaminated. Any porous surface in the room

In 2014, Indiana was the state with the highest number of meth labs and dump sites, with 1,470.[6]

Members of the McMinn County Sheriff Department cleaned up a suspected meth lab in Tennessee in 2004, careful to avoid exposure to what had become a hazardous waste site.

CHILDHOOD DANGERS

In 2017, the US Department of Justice reported on the dangers children face when they live in homes where meth is cooked. The children may become poisoned by inhaling chemicals or eating one of the meth ingredients. Children have died from the toxins they have been exposed to in homes in which meth is cooked. Needles used to inject the drug are also left lying around. Children can be accidentally injected with meth if they pick up discarded needles. In addition, an accidental stick with one of these needles can expose a child to human immunodeficiency virus (HIV), hepatitis, or other potentially deadly viruses carried in the blood.

These children are also more likely to be physically or sexually abused. While coming down off a meth high, their parents may sleep for days. During this time, the children are unsupervised and neglected.

where cooking takes place can also be contaminated. This includes walls, furniture, draperies, blinds, kitchen appliances, lights, fans, vents, and even children's toys.

People who cook meth do not generally worry about how they dispose of this waste. Because of this, extensive areas of contamination can be found outdoors. Officials look for dead vegetation and burned or buried trash. They also check streams, lakes, and sewer systems.

And the result is harm that is undeniable, beginning with the user's brain.

CHAPTER THREE

METH AND THE BRAIN

Meth can be swallowed as a pill or drunk as a liquid. It can be snorted, smoked, or injected. Whichever method people use, their bodies react the same way. The most appealing effect for users is a result of what happens in the brain.

EFFECTS ON DOPAMINE

The brain reacts to meth by releasing a chemical called dopamine. This release causes a feeling of euphoria, or extreme pleasure. Dopamine is naturally released in the brain during pleasurable activities, such as eating junk food. It is also a

Meth causes brain damage from long-term use, including negative changes in structure and function.

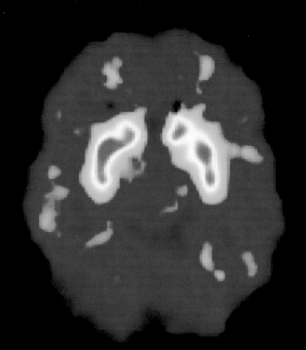

Healthy Control

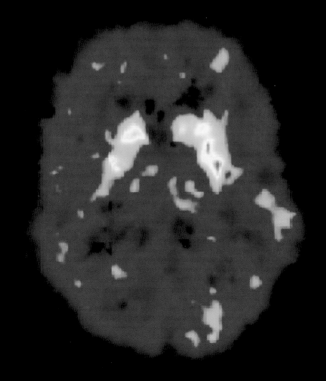

Drug Abuser

common effect of the drugs people abuse. The amount released makes meth unique.

Richard Rawson, a medical doctor and associate director of the University of California, Los Angeles's Integrated Substance Abuse Programs, explained how great the difference is:

> Methamphetamine produces the mother of all dopamine releases. [With] methamphetamine you get a release from the base level to about 1,250 units. Something that's roughly 12 times as much of a release of dopamine as you get from food and sex and other pleasurable activities. This really doesn't occur from any normally rewarding activity. That's one of the reasons why people, when they take methamphetamine, report having this euphoric [feeling] that's unlike anything they've ever experienced.[1]

A meth high can last from 4 to 16 hours.[2] During this high, the person using meth feels smarter than usual and smarter than the people around her. Because of this, the person may start arguments, interrupting people and not letting them speak. When someone is high on meth, the user may also focus intently on something to the point of appearing obsessive. For example, one person who used meth cleaned the same window for several hours. Convincing her that the window was already clean was impossible.

BRAIN DAMAGE

Using meth damages the brain in different ways. One relates to the ability of dopamine receptors to function. Located in the cell membrane, these receptors are what dopamine binds to so it can act on the brain. As the receptors are damaged because of using meth, the brain does not receive dopamine as effectively as it once did. As a result, a person must take more and more meth to achieve the same high.

But dopamine does more than cause a feeling of euphoria. Some dopamine receptors are in the striatum. This part of the brain is associated with memory. When receptors in the striatum function less effectively, meth users experience gaps in their memories. They also struggle to understand abstract concepts and to plan.

Cocaine releases 350 units of dopamine, which is only 28 percent of the amount released by meth.[3]

DOPAMINE

Dopamine plays different roles in the brain. The hormones epinephrine and norepinephrine develop from dopamine. Epinephrine is also called adrenaline. It increases blood pressure and is used to treat heart attacks and allergic reactions. Norepinephrine helps the body prepare to react to a situation the body perceives as dangerous in what is called the fight-or-flight response.

Working in the brain's frontal lobe, which plays a role in motor function, problem-solving, and motivation, dopamine acts as a neurotransmitter. It helps control the flow of information in different parts of the brain. This affects how intensely people feel pleasure and how their brain sends and receives signals that control movement, coordination, emotions, and thought. Researchers have found a link between dopamine and Parkinson's disease, as well as between dopamine and schizophrenia.

HOW METH AFFECTS THE BRAIN

BRAIN

1. When the brain releases dopamine into areas of the brain known as reward pathways, a person feels good.

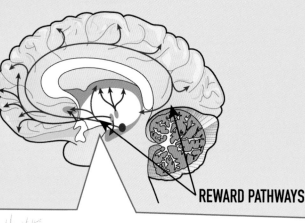

REWARD PATHWAYS

NEURON

CELL BODY

AXON

SYNAPSE

2. Dopamine causes a feeling of pleasure when it moves from one neuron, or brain cell, to another. The dopamine crosses a synapse, or gap, and binds to the next neuron's receptors.

NEXT NEURON

 DOPAMINE

METH

RECEPTORS

3. When a person uses meth, the drug stimulates, or triggers, the brain to release extra amounts of dopamine, creating a feeling of euphoria.

The striatum, which is the main part of the brain affected by meth, is also associated with movement. Using meth causes people to become clumsy. Their problems with movement are similar to the symptoms of Parkinson's disease, which include tremors and slowness. Meth may even contribute to a person developing Parkinson's disease. Some studies have found that people who have used meth show a higher incidence of Parkinson's disease than the general population.

PARANOIA, PSYCHOSIS, AND VIOLENT BEHAVIOR

Meth affects the human brain in other ways as well. As a person uses larger amounts of meth with time, he or she is more likely to hallucinate, be paranoid, or become violent. The repeated use of meth drains the brain's dopamine reserves and damages its ability to produce dopamine. This happens because the human body tries to regulate, or even out, its levels of hormones

POSSIBLE PERMANENT DAMAGE

When she was the director of the National Institute of Drug Abuse, medical doctor Nora Volkow studied X-rays of the brains of several people who had used meth. She found that after not using the drug for 14 months, the abusers' brains had regrown the majority of their damaged dopamine receptors. Despite these new receptors, when tested, these people showed no improvements in motor skills, judgment, or memory. Although brain tissue can regrow, researchers still do not know if any of the lost brain function can or will be recovered.

and other body chemicals. Repeated floods of dopamine generated by meth use cause the body to make less of the chemical. Before long, a user's brain has slightly less dopamine than it had before, and the user needs meth to feel normal.

While dopamine receptors are being damaged, some parts of the human brain are becoming more sensitive to meth. This includes the temporal lobes, the parts of the brain located below the temples. The temporal lobes process sounds and language. These parts of the brain also play a part in processing visual memories. When a person's temporal lobes become sensitized to meth, the person regularly experiences psychosis. These breaks with reality include hallucinations. If the effect is strong enough, the person will hallucinate every time he or she uses meth.

Hallucinations are often accompanied by paranoia. This feeling occurs when meth stimulates the amygdala. When this almond-shaped part of the brain within the temporal lobes

HALLUCINATIONS

Meth-based hallucinations can be visual or auditory. One user reported seeing light flickering out of the corner of her eye as though someone had just entered the room or walked past her. Another user reported being able to see a glittery, cloudlike aura, particles of which she could feel when she passed her hand through it. This person also saw rainbow fingerprints hovering over the surface of her cell phone. Auditory hallucinations include hearing music. One meth user reported hearing helicopters flying overhead and thought the local sheriff was searching for someone. Hallucinations often leave the person feeling irritated, worried, or afraid.

is activated, a person feels fear and anxiety. When a meth user experiences this fear and anxiety because of hallucinations, the person may lash out, causing harm to himself or others.

Another brain chemical released during meth use heightens these sensitivities. Meth causes the brain to release epinephrine, or adrenaline. This hormone is one of the chemicals that activates the body's fight-or-flight response. Adrenaline prepares the body to fight or run away when there is danger. When there is no obvious cause for this chemical release, but there are hallucinations or additional fear and anxiety, violence and psychotic behavior frequently result.

This combination of paranoia, psychosis, and aggression is so common it has a name: meth psychosis. This is the state of mind that occurs when the brain has been exposed too long to too much meth. Stopping meth use does not immediately end meth psychosis. A person who experiences meth psychosis and then quits using meth may continue to have hallucinations and paranoia for months or years. Although these side effects may

METH PARANOIA

Drug counselors point out that many people who use meth claim their food is being poisoned and that they can taste the poison. This is paranoia, and the paranoia caused by meth can last for years. After going five years without meth, one former user still could not use the bathroom without blocking the door. He continued to believe that people might be trying to get him.

disappear when someone stops using meth, stress can cause them to return.

THE TEEN BRAIN

Meth use causes more damage to the teenage brain than to the adult brain. Researchers at the University of Utah and three South Korean universities scanned the brains of 111 South Korean teens and 114 South Korean adults, all of whom used meth.[4]

Ron Bouris lit a candle in honor of Steven, his son. Police officers shot and killed Steven in 2010, when he was swinging an ax in a street in Downey, California, suffering from some of meth's negative effects.

The researchers noted that the area of the brain that supports executive functions was more severely damaged in teens than in adults. Executive functions include mental skills such as logical thinking and impulse control. Other executive functions involve making decisions based on a specific situation and making attainable plans for the future. The researchers' findings confirm the observations doctors have made that meth users suffer from an inability to engage in abstract thought.

In 2011, staff in hospital emergency rooms throughout the United States treated 102,961 people as a result of meth use.[5]

The researchers also noted that all regions of the brains of teens are still developing. The scientists think meth use keeps final connections from forming in the regions responsible for executive functions. The researchers also noted that the teens in the study all tended to take lower doses of meth than the adults. That means a given quantity of meth causes more severe harm in teen users than in adult users.

Meth harms users' brains and mental ability and state regardless of age. But meth's damage goes beyond the brain and psyche.

CHAPTER FOUR

OTHER PHYSICAL EFFECTS

Meth has many physical effects on users other than what happens in the brain. The first effect meth shares with other stimulants. It decreases appetite. A person who uses meth may eat little or nothing for several days. Some people use meth precisely for this reason. They want to lose weight. But long-term meth users often go beyond the point of becoming slim. They become gaunt, looking sickly and skeletal.

When people using meth do feel hungry enough to eat, they frequently make poor food choices. Part of the problem is that they frequently crave sugary foods and drinks. These foods fuel their hyperactive bursts of energy but lack nutritional value.

Law enforcement often publishes mug shots of meth and other drug users, hoping to deter others from using.

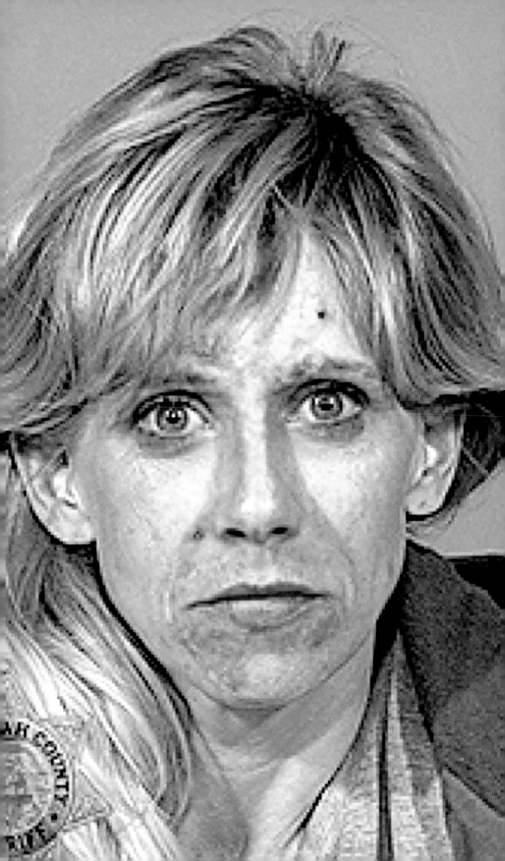

Another effect meth shares with other stimulants is that it keeps people awake. People who are binging on meth may stay awake for several days. They simply do not feel tired. Long periods of wakefulness decrease meth users' ability to make good decisions.

Meth also suppresses the immune system, the bodily system that fights off infections. This diminishes the body's ability to heal itself. Fatigue, weight loss, and slowing the healing response are only some of meth's negative effects on the body. Meth also takes a toll on the cardiovascular system, which is made up of the heart and blood vessels.

USING METH TO LOSE WEIGHT

Many young women use meth because it results in weight loss. One woman, whom reporters called Julie, said she gained 35 pounds (16 kg) after going off the drug.[2] After being clean for several years, Julie started using meth again to lose weight. Bob Hughes, the executive director of ASK Wellness Centre in British Columbia, Canada, who worked with Julie, estimated that 60 percent of his clients who use meth are female. Almost one-third of these women say they used meth to lose weight.[3]

RISKS TO CARDIOVASCULAR HEALTH

Using meth causes a rush common to drug use. The rush from crack cocaine lasts two to five minutes. The rush from meth can last up to 30 minutes.[1]

A big part of the meth rush is the effect the drug has on the heart. It beats faster. Blood pressure goes up as well. These effects can become dangerous. Meth can cause blood pressure to reach unhealthy levels. This can endanger the user's life. Meth can contribute to cardiotoxicity, which is damage or weakness of the heart. Cardiotoxicity can cause arrhythmia, or an irregular heartbeat.

Generally, heart attacks are caused when arteries clogged with fat cannot supply the heart with oxygen-rich blood. Meth use can trigger heart attacks for different reasons. An irregular heartbeat contributes to an irregular blood supply, as can the restricted blood vessels. Without a regular supply of blood, the heart and other organs cannot function properly and may stop working or end up damaged.

Jack Bridges, *left*, cares for his son Shawn, 34, who rests in a hospital bed in his father's house. Meth addiction has ravaged Shawn's body, especially his heart. Jack claims his son has died twice.

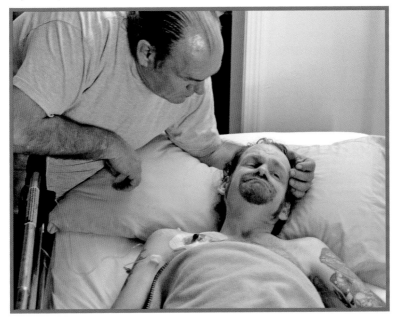

Meth also causes a chemical reaction in the blood that alters proteins. These altered proteins cause inflammation. Antibodies in the bloodstream that normally fight off infections are triggered to attack the altered proteins. These processes damage both the heart and the blood vessels.

Meth causes blood vessels to constrict, or tighten, reducing blood flow. Continual heavy meth use does more than simply constrict the blood vessels. It weakens and kills them. This not only hampers the body's ability to repair itself, but it actually damages tissue. This damage occurs in all parts of the body. Damage to the blood vessels, along with increased heart rate and blood pressure, can lead to a stroke, too. A stroke occurs when blood flow to part of the brain is interrupted. As with a heart attack, this can occur because a blood vessel is clogged or damaged. Meth's effects make a stroke more likely.

A 2017 US study showed that methamphetamine addicts were 3.7 times more likely to have heart failure or chronic heart disease than people who had not taken meth.[4]

The majority of deaths due to meth use are a result of either heart attacks or strokes. When first responders arrive on the scene of a meth emergency, there is nothing they can do about the meth the person has already taken. All they can do is focus on treating the symptoms. They try to restart the heart, stabilize the heartbeat, or restore blood flow to the brain. Although the heartbeat may be restored, damage to the heart may be irreversible and may contribute to heart failure, as the damaged heart is unable to pump enough blood through the body.

MUSCLE FAILURE

Meth is also fatal when it leads to rhabdomyolysis, a breakdown of muscle tissue that can lead to kidney failure. Meth is hard on the kidneys in several ways. The high blood pressure and damaged blood vessels meth use causes can harm the kidneys.

Another problem is that people who are using meth often have fevers. A higher-than-normal body temperature can cause a person to become dehydrated, a condition caused by lack of water in the body. If the person is binging on meth and not drinking water, this worsens the problem. When the body does not have enough water, it does not function properly. Organs, including the kidneys, can shut down.

Chronic fever does even more damage when it is paired with the muscle twitching sometimes experienced by those who use meth. The heat and constant motion together damage the muscle fibers. Accumulated damage can cause the muscle fibers to break down, which floods the body with toxins. In trying to filter out these toxins, the already weakened kidneys shut down.

Like heart failure, kidney failure can be irreversible. This is because severely damaged kidneys can no longer filter toxins from the body. If this inability to function is caught in time, the person can undergo dialysis. In one type of dialysis, the blood is filtered and purified by a machine. The process takes up to four hours to complete and must be done three times per week. Complete kidney failure may also require a kidney transplant, but that is not always possible because doctors must find a suitable donor. Without treatment or a transplant, a person will die.

SKIN DAMAGE

The damage meth does to blood vessels is often first obvious in the skin. The person's face loses muscle. Skin becomes less elastic and sags. A meth user's skin also looks less healthy, becoming dull and somewhat gray. People who use meth age prematurely

During dialysis, a machine does the work of the kidneys. Blood travels from the patient's arm to the dialysis machine and back into the patient's arm.

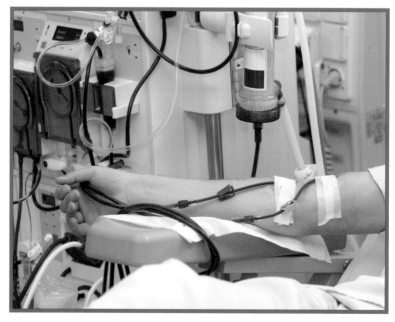

and look much older than they are. Health-care professionals often refer to this damage and the changes in appearance that it causes as premature aging.

People using meth often become prone to acne. Their skin breaks out, and the acne does not heal. In part, this is because they pick at themselves to get rid of the insects they hallucinate are crawling on and under their skin, creating sores that become infected. Some of these infections increase in size, becoming ulcers, which are open wounds.

HYPERTHERMIA

Meth users can also suffer from hyperthermia, which can be one of the most damaging symptoms of a meth overdose. Hyperthermia means a person's body temperature is elevated.

THE POWER OF PHOTOGRAPHY

One rehab website displays "The Horrors of Methamphetamines," a gallery of photographs of meth users. The images show the dramatic effects of the drug on each user's appearance. Some people in the gallery have only one photo labeled with their age. Most of the people have multiple photos. One is from before they started using meth or early in their drug use. The others are from during the time the person used meth. Each photo is labeled with the person's age, showing the toll of using meth. Symbols indicate the physical effects the user experienced, which include skin damage, dental damage, and premature aging.

Some people have questioned the website for doing this, claiming the gallery focuses on physical attractiveness. But the site's owners hoped seeing the damage meth causes would help viewers understand. A survey of viewers found that almost 52 percent thought the photos did not cause unfair prejudice against the people portrayed but showed clearly the damage done by meth use.[5]

10 Years of Meth Us[e]

The effects of meth on a user's appearance can make the person almost unrecognizable in a short period of time.

Doctors diagnose a person with hyperthermia when his or her temperature is higher than 101.3 degrees Fahrenheit (38.5°C). Most often, hyperthermia is a summertime danger. This is because it can occur when someone exercises, works, or plays a sport outside in the heat. Hyperthermia also happens

when someone lives in a home without air-conditioning and experiences hot weather. Prolonged exposure to extremely high temperatures raises the person's body temperature.

Hyperthermia is dangerous because a series of complex chemical reactions enable the human body to operate. These reactions require a certain temperature, normally between 98 and 100 degrees Fahrenheit (37 to 38°C). When someone's body temperature is too high, these necessary reactions cannot occur or occur too quickly.

In 2003, the *Journal of Neuroscience* published the results of a study showing that even small doses of meth can cause a person's brain and body temperatures to increase. Researchers found that in meth-induced hyperthermia, the brain temperature is normally higher than the body temperature. The overall rise in temperature can last three to five hours.[6] This prolonged high temperature damages the brain through the breakdown of proteins, tissue inflammation, and bleeding. Prolonged hyperthermia can also lead to convulsions. The convulsions, in turn, can lead to muscle breakdown and even rhabdomyolysis. Someone who overdoses on meth and suffers from hyperthermia needs to receive immediate medical attention.

RISKS TO ORAL HEALTH

The premature aging meth users experience is worsened by another side effect, known as meth mouth. This is one of the most recognizable physical signs of meth use. Meth mouth is characterized by rotten, ground-down teeth. Doctors and researchers are still looking for the exact cause. One factor is that people using meth habitually grind their teeth. This wears down their enamel, the protective outer layer of the tooth. Without this protection, teeth are more prone to cavities and decay.

The ingredients of meth may also play a role in meth mouth. Researchers have reported on the corrosive properties of the anhydrous ammonia, red phosphorous, and lithium. When meth is smoked or snorted, the corrosive effects of these chemicals may further erode the teeth.

More recent research shows the corrosive effects of these chemicals are likely made more severe by another effect of meth. As the drug constricts and kills blood vessels, blood vessels in the mouth die. Tissues in the mouth die as well, which quickly increases dental damage.

A meth user who visited the University of Kentucky College of Dentistry showed signs of meth mouth. Meth dries out saliva, which is important in keeping teeth from rotting.

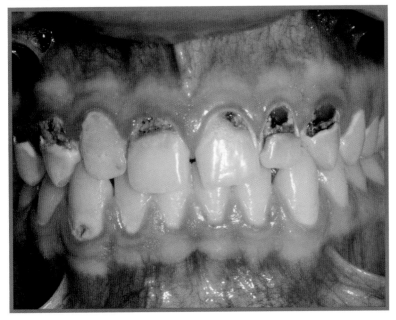

One final side effect of meth use is xerostomia, or dry mouth. Saliva normally dilutes and neutralizes the acids found in the mouth. When a person develops dry mouth, the acids are no longer diluted and can eat away at the teeth and gums. This leads to weak spots in the teeth where cavities can easily form. The formation of cavities and breakdown of teeth is worsened by teeth grinding and binging on sugary foods. All of these various side effects contribute to meth mouth.

BAD BREATH

Chronic meth use causes halitosis, or bad breath. A large part of the problem is meth mouth. Rotten teeth smell bad. Even before full-blown meth mouth develops, acute necrotizing ulcerative gingivitis can contribute to the problem. This is the medical term for damaged gums that are inflamed and sore. The gingivitis is caused by bad dental hygiene compounded by stress. In extreme cases, the person has ulcers on the gums. The sickness can actually be smelled.

The potential physical and mental harm of using meth are only some of the risks people take when using the drug. Some users suffer effects that go beyond their body and themselves.

NEGATIVE EFFECTS

The negative effects of using meth range from mild, such as dry mouth, to severe and even deadly, such as organ damage and heart attack.

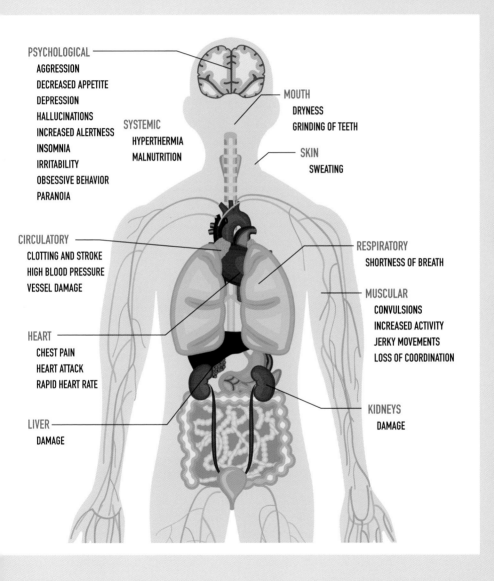

PSYCHOLOGICAL
- AGGRESSION
- DECREASED APPETITE
- DEPRESSION
- HALLUCINATIONS
- INCREASED ALERTNESS
- INSOMNIA
- IRRITABILITY
- OBSESSIVE BEHAVIOR
- PARANOIA

SYSTEMIC
- HYPERTHERMIA
- MALNUTRITION

MOUTH
- DRYNESS
- GRINDING OF TEETH

SKIN
- SWEATING

CIRCULATORY
- CLOTTING AND STROKE
- HIGH BLOOD PRESSURE
- VESSEL DAMAGE

RESPIRATORY
- SHORTNESS OF BREATH

MUSCULAR
- CONVULSIONS
- INCREASED ACTIVITY
- JERKY MOVEMENTS
- LOSS OF COORDINATION

HEART
- CHEST PAIN
- HEART ATTACK
- RAPID HEART RATE

KIDNEYS
- DAMAGE

LIVER
- DAMAGE

CHAPTER FIVE

PERSONAL EFFECTS

People choose to use meth for a variety of reasons. Some try it because friends or family members use meth. Others want to dull emotional or mental pain. Still others want to feel good for a while. No matter why someone uses meth for the first time, most people use it again because meth provides a high like no other. But the high does not and cannot last forever. Eventually, the user must come off the high. And for those who become addicted to the drug, meth can affect their lives and the people around them. Abusing meth can cause lives to crash.

Renee DeMontreux dropped out of college soon after she started using meth. Now clean, she works at a rehab facility helping others overcome addiction.

BINGING AND TWEAKING

Although meth provides a high like no other drug, eventually the high wears off. This is known as crashing. Because crashing feels so awful, people who use a drug may try to keep the high going by taking more of it. This abuse of the drug, called binging, is not unique to meth use. People also binge on things such as food and alcohol.

Someone who has been using meth may go on a type of binge known as a "run."[1] During a run, when the high starts to fade, the person will use more meth. They do this again and again to delay the crash, but each consecutive high is lower than the one before.

During a run, the person using meth is mentally and physically hyperactive. They are intense and energetic, but this energy is largely fueled by meth, because many people on a run do not eat or sleep. Binging often lasts three to 15 days.[2] During

OBSESSING BECAUSE OF METH

Obsessive behavior during meth use can take many forms. One woman spent time on her computer changing the settings on various programs so they would run faster. When computers no longer interested her, she obsessed about dumpster diving, "rescuing" audio equipment behind Radio Shack and pens behind Office Depot.[3] Another woman trimmed her hair repeatedly until it was very short. Some people take things apart. Police have reported knowing a location is used as a meth house because the washing machine is disassembled on the front lawn.

this time, the user may take meth as often as every few hours. Eventually, even with more meth, there is no rush and no high.

When a user can no longer get high, they enter the next phase of the meth experience. Sometimes, this period is called the "come-down" or "low" because the person is coming down off the high.[4] This terminology is common among drug use in general. When discussing meth specifically, this period is often called "tweaking."[5]

Drug abuse experts often consider tweaking the most dangerous phase of meth use. This is because when people are coming off a high, they crave more meth because they want that high back. But they already used so much meth they simply cannot get high. Because of this, they feel empty and desperate.

METH PSYCHOSIS AND LAW ENFORCEMENT

Someone who is tweaking is likely to react violently if confronted. Drug counselors have noted that someone tweaking often reacts negatively to the sight of a police uniform. This can be compounded by the fact that a police officer may not know someone is tweaking. People who are drunk slur their speech and often smell like alcohol. Meth use has no such indicators. It is also easy to confuse someone having meth psychosis with someone who has schizophrenia, a mental illness characterized by hallucinations and unusual ways of thinking. Because police officers respond to 911 calls when someone acts irrationally, it is important for them to distinguish between someone who is using meth and may become violent and someone who has schizophrenia and is unlikely to do something violent.

Tweaking has physical symptoms. Itching is the most common. Fever and convulsions are common as well.

People who are tweaking often have psychotic symptoms. They lose touch with reality. What they think they feel and observe is not real. When this happens, they may think the itching they are feeling is because bugs are crawling under or over their skin. These psychotic breaks are strengthened by the fact that these people often have not slept for days. As they become exhausted, they tend to hallucinate, believing imaginary

A woman named Sandy cares for her brother, Ricky. Much of Ricky's body was burned when his meth lab exploded. He was in bed after being awake for several days because of meth.

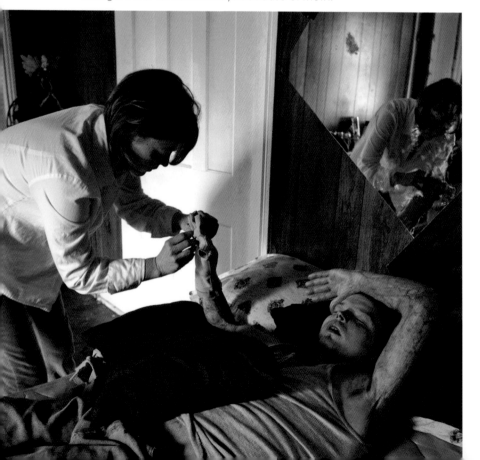

things they see and hear are real. People who are tweaking may be irrationally afraid, believing someone is after them or wants to hurt them. Because of these psychoses, people who are tweaking are often a danger to themselves and to those around them.

Eventually, the person is completely exhausted and crashes. When this happens, the user falls asleep for one to three days. The person sleeps so soundly that he or she appears almost lifeless.

ADDICTION

For some users, this becomes their life. They become addicted. As with any addiction, the physical and emotional dependence the person has on meth can lead to a wide variety of damaging behaviors. Many people who use meth find themselves leading a double life.

This was especially true for Allison Moore. In 2004, the Hawaii resident joined the Maui Police Department and became a police officer. The job was tough, but she loved working the 12-hour days required of her job. But following problems with her married boyfriend, Moore was feeling depressed. When a fellow officer dropped a bag of meth on her desk to be cataloged as evidence, she pocketed the drug. Moore explained what happened:

I carried the drugs around for the rest of the week. And on
Saturday, my day off, I sat in my bedroom with the blinds

drawn and stared at the baggy. I was so desperate for
anything to make me feel better . . . and it would just be this
one time. I poured out a few of the clear, tiny crystals, and
even though you're supposed to smoke it, I snorted it. I felt it
burn in my nostrils and my eyes teared up. But then, I felt the
most amazing, ecstatic high I'd ever felt. My life felt livable; I
felt happy.[6]

Moore knew right away she would take more meth. "I knew I
had to do it again," she said.[7] But she also had a problem because
she was a police officer specializing in narcotics. Because she
arrested dealers and users, the local dealers knew who she was,
so she had to travel out of the area where she worked to buy the
drugs she craved:

Once a month, I'd fly to Honolulu and stay for a few hours—
long enough to drive around looking for a prostitute to lead
me to her dealer and get my supply. I was so brazen, I'd carry
the drugs in my pants pockets when I boarded the plane
home. Because I had a badge, I felt invincible.[8]

Lying quickly becomes a way of life for many people who
are using meth. Moore took pains to hide the changes meth was
making in her appearance. She bought colored contact lenses
so no one could see that her pupils were dilated or enlarged,
a common indicator of a meth high. But fellow police officers
noticed she had lost weight. Moore lied and told them she had
ovarian cancer. When Moore left town to hide her meth use, she

told coworkers she was staying with family while being treated for cancer. One fellow officer organized a fund-raiser to help pay for her treatments.

STEALING WHAT THEY NEED

As a person develops an addiction to meth, all he or she thinks about is getting more of the drug. Moore was no exception. "Being a single workaholic before I started using, I'd stockpiled a nice little nest egg of about $35,000. In a few months, that was gone on plane tickets and meth."[9] At that point, she started skimming meth from drug busts to feed her habit.

But theft is not limited to meth itself. Some people break into pharmacies to steal the ingredients to make meth. Others steal money from family and friends and use the cash to buy meth. Still other people steal things they can sell to buy drugs. In 2015, in Fenton, Missouri, Steven Fisher drove to Walmart and loaded three televisions into his car without paying for them.

STEALING IDENTITIES

Some people steal identities to pay for their meth. "Ninety percent of our ID theft cases deal with drugs," said Steve Williams, a police detective in Eugene, Oregon, who told interviewers the drug is usually meth.[10] In identity theft, people steal personal information and use it to obtain credit cards and cash. Those who run ID theft rings employ meth users because meth keeps them awake for days sorting stolen mail and piecing together shredded documents. In 2000, Steven Massey, the operator of one Eugene ring, was convicted for stealing approximately $400,000.[11]

Several days later, he returned to the store and stole more items. When police officers arrested him, Fisher confessed that he had taken these things to support his meth habit.

SEX AND NEEDLES

Theft is not always enough to feed a meth habit. After she moved in with her sister in Seattle, Washington, Moore started trading sex for meth, finding men through the website Craigslist. "When I realized those trades weren't getting me enough meth, I prostituted for money, which I'd use to get ice from dealers," Moore said.[12]

When someone on meth is having sex for money, the problem often becomes one of safety. "You do things when you're on meth that you would never do sober," said Peter Staley, a former meth user. "Condoms? Forget about it."[13]

The risks of unprotected sex go beyond unwanted pregnancy. Unprotected sex can also result in getting sexually transmitted infections. In addition, many meth users inject the drug. Some users share needles, which puts them at risk for human immunodeficiency virus (HIV) and hepatitis. HIV compromises the immune system, and a person who has it can lose the ability to fight off other illnesses. Hepatitis is a liver infection that can cause inflammation of this organ and even lead to liver cancer. Both viruses are spread through contact with infected blood or other body fluids. So, even if a meth user never shares needles, having unprotected sex puts that person at risk for contracting these diseases from a sex partner.

AFFECTING OTHERS

Meth use also affects people in the user's life, including those who are closest to the user. People with addictions risk their most personal relationships, including with spouses or partners and with their children. The addiction consumes users' lives. It makes people not follow through on promises or commitments. Trust can become an issue, too, especially when the

CHILDREN AT RISK

Few studies have been done on the effects of meth on unborn babies. Doctors have seen that pregnant women who take meth have babies who are born early and smaller than normal and who have smaller-than-average skulls. Doctors pay special attention to skull size because it correlates with brain size and brain development. Babies born to women using meth also have a higher-than-average rate of cleft, or split, lip and gastroschisis, which is being born with a loop of intestine sticking out through a hole near the navel. These children often have trouble swallowing and problems breathing. They are also sensitive to touch.

Children who grow up in homes where meth is made or used are at risk from meth on the floors, furniture, and their clothing as well as the fumes when meth is smoked. Brief exposure to a small amount of meth may cause headaches, nausea, or dizziness. Exposure to a large amount of meth may cause a cough and breathing problems. Children may become dizzy, suffer from a lack of coordination, and have chemical burns on their skin. Prolonged exposure can be fatal.

In Riverside, California, Manuel Fuentes of Child Protective Services explains to Julie Beth Rossiter he will be taking her children after police found a meth lab at the house where the family was living.

user lies to and steals from his or her family and friends. And if stealing leads to jail time, the user disappears from everyday life for his or her loved ones, possibly for decades.

Addiction also affects people's work lives. Getting and keeping a job is unlikely for them. They can be problematic for the companies that employ them. Workers who use drugs sometimes steal from their employers to support their drug habit. This is a financial drain on businesses. These workers cost their employers in other ways, including by missing work or by not being productive while at work. These employees might also use their health insurance more, which also costs their employers money.

BREAKING THE HABIT

It often takes a crisis to get someone to stop using meth. Moore left her sister's home to live with her boyfriend, who was a drug dealer. Moore's boyfriend held her prisoner, but eventually she figured out his computer password and emailed her mother for help. Moore's mother took her to a rehab center in Taos, New Mexico, where she got the treatment she needed.

Melanda Adams was cooking meth in a rural Kentucky lab in 2004 when the police knocked on the door. She had realized how hopeless her life had become and that no one, friends or family, wanted anything to do with her. The arrest gave her the opportunity to seek treatment. She credits the police officers with saving her life.

QUITTING METH

Once someone decides to quit using meth, the person also has to decide how to do it. The user can quit cold, which means she completely quits using meth all at once. She can also taper, which means using less and less through time. Whichever method a user chooses, the person will have to cope with withdrawal.

PHYSICAL SYMPTOMS

The physical symptoms of meth withdrawal include headache, fatigue, and exhaustion. Because people using meth sleep and eat very little, the first week or two of withdrawal is sometimes called the "sleep, drink, and eat stage."[1] Many people going through withdrawal comment on how much sleep

Stacy "Fergie" Ferguson, lead singer of the Black Eyed Peas, was once addicted to meth. She described giving up the drug: "It was the hardest boyfriend I ever had to break up with."[2]

they seem to need. Even after waking, the person will still feel exhausted physically, mentally, and emotionally.

Some people who are recovering from meth use gain weight during this time. If they took meth to be slender, the weight gain may be frustrating. It can take up to two months before the person's metabolism and sleep pattern return to normal. The mental and emotional side effects of withdrawal are more serious than the physical ones.

MENTAL SYMPTOMS

Although the symptoms of meth withdrawal last for much longer than a day, the worst phase is the first 24 hours. During this time, the symptoms peak. Although the physical symptoms are not harmful or dangerous, some emotional symptoms can be. They include panic, anxiety, and depression. The feelings can be so strong they lead to suicidal thoughts. Much of the problem comes from the fact that meth elevates dopamine levels and damages dopamine receptors. As a result, the person who stops using meth may feel no pleasure. Everyday activities

---

TWO WAYS TO OVERDOSE

There are two types of meth overdose. An acute overdose is a sudden overdose. It occurs when the person uses a large quantity of meth at once. The person's body cannot handle the strain created by taking so much of the stimulant at one time. A chronic overdose occurs over a longer period, when the negative effects of frequent and constant use of meth add up. Both types of overdose can cause a heart attack or a stroke and result in death.

the person used to enjoy have no positive effect. Instead, the person feels depressed and anxious. As the body tries to return to normal, repairing receptors and again producing normal amounts of dopamine, the person may experience extreme mood swings. For some people, emotional lows involve uncontrollable tears. Some former users have reported crying when they hear a certain song. Other recovering users experience intense anger. They are so on edge they are likely to snap at anyone who speaks to them.

TOO MUCH METH

How much meth it takes to overdose varies according to the size and weight of the person taking it, other drugs the person has taken, the person's overall health, and how the drug is used. Recovery experts say anyone who smokes or snorts approximately 0.002 ounces (50 mg) or more of meth is at risk for overdosing. A person who injects meth risks overdosing when using more than approximately 0.003 ounces (100 mg). Finally, anyone who takes meth tablets or drinks the drug dissolved in a beverage risks overdosing at approximately 0.005 ounces (150 mg) per day.[3]

Because many people who are in withdrawal are exhausted and depressed, they continue to crave meth. Some of them want to feel the high meth brings. Others think a chemical nudge will help them regain enough energy to act like a normal person. Whatever the reason, the cravings are real and can last four to five weeks. Because this period is so draining, many people

CRYSTAL METH WITHDRAWAL TIMELINE

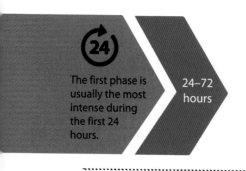

24–72 hours

The first phase is usually the most intense during the first 24 hours.

- Feel exhausted
- May experience extreme anxiety, panic, and suicidal thoughts
- Paranoia and hallucinations possible

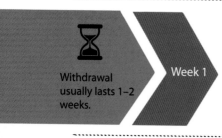

Week 1

Withdrawal usually lasts 1–2 weeks.

- Strong meth cravings can appear
- May experience feelings of hopelessness
- Poor concentration, aches, pains, and headaches also common
- Rapid weight gain may be triggered

Week 2

Symptoms can last up to four weeks.

- Likely to still experience mood swings, depression, and other symptoms

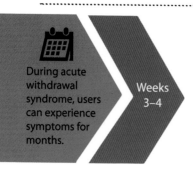

Weeks 3–4

During acute withdrawal syndrome, users can experience symptoms for months.

- Should start to feel much better after a month
- Mood should settle
- Sleep pattern should return to normal
- Energy levels will improve

will use meth again to relieve these feelings. This makes going through withdrawal at home alone very difficult.

WITHDRAWING WITHOUT MEDICAL HELP

Some people will try to go through withdrawal on their own, without any medical help. Sometimes, they do not want to ask for help because they are embarrassed about having become addicted to meth. Other times, they simply do not have the money needed to pay for treatment, which can reach $60,000 for a three-month program.[4]

Detoxing at home can be difficult. For some people, the problem is that they used meth at home with a family member, a boyfriend or girlfriend, or a roommate. When this is the case, the temptation to use again is always present.

During detox, the greatest danger a meth user faces is dehydration.

Quitting at home can also be challenging if the person has been using more than one drug. Many heroin users also use meth, which means the person has to detox from heroin and meth at the same time.

Detoxing at home can also be problematic if the meth user has a dual diagnosis. This means the person has a drug addiction that is fueled by a mental health problem such as an eating disorder, anxiety, or depression. When a person with a dual diagnosis goes through withdrawal, he must deal with

Jeremy, 19, has been in drug treatment six times, four of which were for meth use, and he is losing hope that he will beat his addiction.

problems associated with his mental health issues as well as end his addiction to meth. Detoxing without the support of a mental health professional can make getting through the process particularly difficult.

Whether or not any of these problems exist for an individual, a person who is trying to stop using meth and going through withdrawal should always have someone else present in case she needs help. This might include reminding the person to eat and

drink. Or a counselor could be present to talk the person through problems associated with depression or anxiety, providing encouragement and reminding the person she is not alone.

TREATMENT OPTIONS

Various treatment options are available for users who want to stop taking meth. The most effective treatments for meth addiction so far have been behavioral therapies.

UNDERSTANDING AND COPING WITH TRIGGERS

Anything that makes a person recall his or her meth use can be a trigger. This is because thinking about meth use generally makes the person crave meth and can encourage the individual to use it again. A trigger can be external, or something outside of the person. External triggers might include smells associated with meth use. If a person used meth at parties, triggers could be smells that remind the person of parties, such as cigarette smoke. Sounds, such as dance music, can also act as triggers.

Some triggers are internal and include the person's thoughts and emotions. Some internal triggers make the person feel bad, such as thinking about someone who died. Others revolve around feeling good and make the person want to feel that way again. After identifying triggers, the individual has to learn to avoid or disarm them. This can mean making new friends, learning to redirect negative thoughts to something more positive, or doing something new and exciting, such as traveling or playing a favorite sport.

Cognitive behavioral therapy involves helping the person identify negative thought patterns and patterns of behavior. Working with a therapist, the recovering user identifies triggers, which are the things that make the person want to use meth. Triggers can include being around a sibling who uses meth or always using meth after going to a party with certain friends. Triggers can also be situations or people who make the person feel bad about himself or herself. Whatever the triggers are for an individual, the therapist helps the person find a way to avoid or cope with them. This could mean finding a new place to live, making new friends, or avoiding certain clubs.

Contingency-management intervention has also been helpful in treating people who use meth. This type of therapy involves offering patients concrete incentives not to use meth. Incentives can include money, privileges within the clinic or treatment facility, or restaurant vouchers for every clean drug test. These incentives may seem trivial, but studies have found that programs that use these incentives help patients stay off meth. What works best will vary from person to person, and a trained therapist or other medical professional can help a person in recovery figure out what strategy to use. This is critical because using meth can result in serious legal consequences.

Some experts say up to 93 percent of people who have used meth will return to using the drug after treatment.[5]

CHAPTER SEVEN

LEGAL CONSEQUENCES

The Drug Enforcement Administration (DEA) is the US government agency that investigates drug-related crimes in the United States. As part of its mission, the DEA maintains a list of drugs that ranks them based on their danger and the severity of their legal consequences. Drugs are classified into five schedules, or categories. The purpose of this list is to make passing legislation easier at the state level. When a state passes a drug law, the text does not have to list every drug to which

An officer arrests a man for having drug paraphernalia after the man tried to buy more cold medicine than legal limits allow.

RACE, DRUGS, AND PRISON SENTENCES

There is a racial difference between who uses drugs and who goes to jail on drug charges. A 2009 report by the Bureau of Justice Statistics found that whites are more likely than blacks to have used most illegal drugs, while blacks are more likely than whites to go to prison because of drugs. Jamie Fellner, who wrote the report, said of the racial disparity, "The race issue isn't just that the judge is going, 'Oh, black man, I'm gonna sentence you higher.' The police go into low-income minority neighborhoods and that's where they make most of their drug arrests. If they arrest you, now you have a 'prior,' so if you plead or get arrested again, you're gonna have a higher sentence. There's a kind of cumulative effect."[1]

Serving prison time can have lasting effects. People who have served time on a felony charge can lose out on money from the federal government for housing and for financial aid. And some might be denied employment because potential employers often require job applicants to note any criminal history.

the law applies but instead includes the appropriate schedule from the DEA's list. A drug can also be added to a particular category without having to rewrite laws in every state.

Many Schedule 1 drugs, including heroin, are the most addictive and have no medical uses. The exception is marijuana, which is used to treat pain. Schedule 5 drugs, which include prescription cough suppressants and mild prescription pain relievers, are the least addictive and have medical uses. They might be abused if not used under the direction of a doctor. Meth is a Schedule 2 drug. Schedule 2 drugs are highly addictive, physically and mentally, but they have medical uses. For example, meth can be prescribed for attention deficit hyperactivity disorder, which is commonly referred to as ADHD. Having meth without a doctor's prescription can bring severe legal penalties.

If someone is arrested for possession of meth, the penalty he or she faces depends on the amount and purity of the drug. A person might be charged with a misdemeanor, which is a minor offense, or a felony, which is a major offense. Usually, possession of meth results in a felony with harsh punishments, though this can vary from state to state. There is one set of penalties if the drug is pure and the person had between 0.2 and 1.7 ounces (5–49 g) or the drug is a mixture and the person had between 1.8 and 17.6 ounces (50–499 g). If it is a first offense—the first time the person was arrested for possession of a controlled substance—the individual can be sent to prison for 5 to 40 years. If it is a second offense, the prison term is 10 years to life. In addition, punishment includes a fine of up to $5 million for a first offense and up to $10 million for a second offense.[2]

If the person had 1.8 ounces (50 g) or more of pure meth or 17.6 ounces (500 g) or more of a mixture, the penalties go up. For a first offense, the person faces 10 years to life in prison. For a second offense, the prison sentence is 20 years to life. The monetary penalty is up to $10 million for a first offense and $20 million for a second offense. If someone gets parole, or early release from prison, and is arrested again for possession of

STATE PENALTIES

In addition to the federal laws imposed on Schedule 2 drugs, people who are arrested in possession of meth also face state laws and penalties. When a person is convicted, the penalties for breaking state laws are added to the penalties for breaking federal laws. In Illinois, for example, these penalties are more specific, with different charges for manufacturing, possession with the intent to sell, and possession to traffic, or transport. The maximum charge for manufacturing meth in Illinois is 60 years in prison and a fine of up to $400,000. The maximum charge for the delivery or intent to deliver meth in Illinois is 60 years in prison and a fine of up to $400,000. The maximum charge for trafficking meth in Illinois is 120 years in prison and a fine of up to $400,000 when the amount is more than 32 ounces (900 g).[4]

meth, the penalties are fixed at life in prison and a fine of up to $20 million.[3]

A NEW LAW LIMITS AMOUNTS

Sending people to prison and making them pay fines did not curb the meth epidemic of the 1980s and 1990s. Seeking another solution, lawmakers decided to focus legislation on an ingredient that is essential to making meth. They would regulate pseudoephedrine.

On March 9, 2006, President George W. Bush signed the USA Patriot Act. Title VII of this law is the Combat Methamphetamine Act of 2005. The Patriot Act is best known for enabling law enforcement to respond to threats of terrorism. Making the Combat Methamphetamine Act part of the larger Patriot Act enabled law enforcement and intelligence agencies to exchange information. The goal

US senator Dianne Feinstein displayed the new daily limit a person can buy of cold medicine, an ingredient in meth, during a news conference on December 14, 2005.

was to increase national security while giving the government the tools necessary to combat both threats. The Combat Methamphetamine Act limits the sale of all cough, cold, and allergy products that contain pseudoephedrine. It requires shoppers to show photo identification, such as a driver's license, to buy anything containing pseudoephedrine. Pharmacies also must keep lists of who buys which pseudoephedrine products and how much they buy.

The amount is critical because the law limits the amount of pseudoephedrine a person can buy per day to

0.13 ounces (3.6 g).[5] It does not matter whether the person is buying pseudoephedrine tablets or pseudoephedrine in combination with other cold-fighting ingredients. It also does not matter whether two people in the same home are sick or have a doctor's prescription. The law sets a hard limit.

The same law also imposes a monthly limit of 0.32 ounces (9 g) for both products. Mail-order companies are limited to 0.26 ounces (7.5 g) of pseudoephedrine per customer within 30 days.[6] Because of these limits, pharmaceutical companies had to change how they packaged cold and allergy remedies.

These limits enforced by the DEA mean cold and allergy remedies containing pseudoephedrine can no longer be stocked on pharmacy and grocery store shelves. Instead, they are in the pharmacy or inside a locked cabinet or shelf in the store. These items are now available only during pharmacy hours, even if someone is sick and in need of the relief pseudoephedrine provides.

NOT WITHOUT A PRESCRIPTION

Following the first laws regulating pseudoephedrine, meth use tapered off, but only temporarily. It then resurged. Some lawmakers think the best way to combat this upswing is to pass new, more restrictive laws. They want to make pseudoephedrine available only with a doctor's prescription.

By 2017, two states had passed such laws: Oregon in 2006 and Mississippi in 2010.[7] Politicians in various state legislatures have introduced other bills that would make pseudoephedrine available by prescription only. Sixteen of these bills were introduced in 2013 alone. None of these additional attempts at legislation have passed.

With so many states unable to pass more restrictive laws, various cities have put their own laws into effect. In Missouri, the cities of Branson, Cape Girardeau, and Joplin require prescriptions to buy pseudoephedrine. In Tennessee, the cities of Estill Springs, Huntland, and Winchester have passed prescription-only laws, too.

A 2013 Government Accountability Office report asserts that the laws are working to reduce the effects of meth. The report points to the number of meth lab incidents in Oregon and Mississippi, the only two states with prescription-only requirements for pseudoephedrine. In 2005, the year before Oregon passed its prescription-only law, the state had 232 meth lab incidents. In 2011, there were 11. Mississippi has also seen a decline, dropping from 937 in 2010 to 321 in 2011.[9] A reduction in meth lab incidents means a reduction in pollutants and the resources required to deal with cleanup as well as the health risk to emergency personnel. Authorities hoped this drop would correspond with a drop in use, but the demand for this drug is now being filled by meth brought into the country from Mexico.

STRAINED PRISON RESOURCES

Meth is taking a toll in areas other than law enforcement and cleanup costs. Prison resources are also under strain due to the number of incarcerated people who have or had addictions to meth. Dentists who work in prisons and jails report an increase in the numbers of problems they must treat that are related to meth mouth. In August 2005, a National Public Radio (NPR) report stated that Minnesota Department of Corrections dental costs had doubled since 2000. This was mostly due to the extensive dental work performed on meth addicts.

Chris Heringlake, a dentist at St. Cloud Correctional Facility in Minnesota, told NPR reporters he first saw meth mouth in the late 1990s. By 2005, he was seeing cases of it every day. In this same 2005 report, Athena Bettger, a dentist at the Multnomah County Jail in Portland, Oregon, agreed:

The general trend that I am seeing is that there is a definite increase. There are more and more teeth that need assistance and there are more and more [inmates] needing assistance.[10]

But the criminal justice costs of meth extend to more than the dental health-care costs of inmates. In 2009, the Rand Corporation, a research organization that gathers information to enable better public policy decisions, estimated the costs of meth use in the United States in 2005. The total estimated

At the Cuyahoga County jail, dental hygiene technician Sally Wright, *right,* speaks with an inmate.

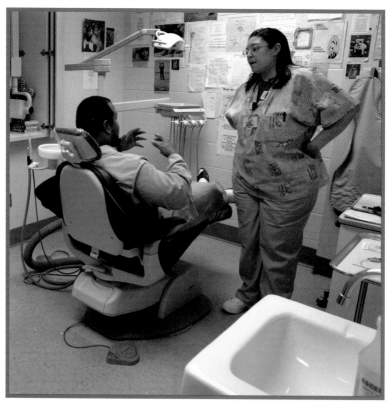

criminal justice cost in 2005 was $4.2 billion. Legal fees required to process people for possession and use of meth were approximately $2.1 billion. Fees to process people for violent crimes and property crimes committed while on meth or trying to find meth cost taxpayers $1.8 billion. Processing

In 2015, meth users accounted for 24 percent of the drug offenders sent to US federal prisons.[12]

people for parole and revoking parole for probation offenses cost another $70 million.[11] The costs of dealing with meth continue to mount because the epidemic has not gone away. It has simply changed. While production of meth in the United States dropped off, imported meth continued to feed the addictions of US users. And although changes in the availability of pseudoephedrine led to a decrease in meth production in the United States, the epidemic soon had a new supply from south of the border. Meth produced in Mexico and brought into the United States had launched a new, deadlier phase in America's meth epidemic.

THE CURRENT SITUATION

With restrictions on pseudoephedrine established in the mid-2000s, the manufacturing of meth in large labs tapered off throughout the United States. From 2004 to 2005, authorities in Jefferson County, Missouri, raided two or three meth labs a day. News stories frequently called the area the meth capital of the world. But in 2016, after laws restricting pseudoephedrine were established, a Missouri Highway Patrol database listed only

Officers seized these pills containing pseudoephedrine during a 2010 raid.

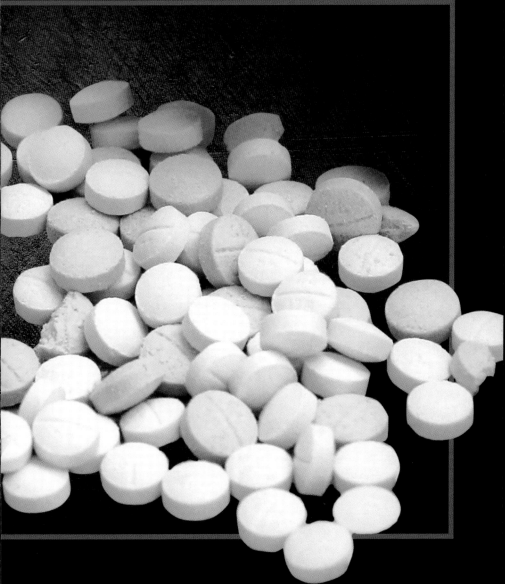

51 meth lab busts for the county. This drop was not limited to Jefferson County. Neighboring Franklin County had 139 meth lab busts in 2004 and only four in 2016.[1] "It's back to being newsworthy if you find a meth lab," said Jason Grellner, a former Franklin County Sheriff's Department lieutenant who made a career for himself by busting local meth labs.[2]

The number of meth labs being busted may have dropped in Missouri and other parts of the United States, but meth use has actually increased nationwide. According to the Substance Abuse and Mental Health Services Administration (SAMHSA), between 2010 and 2015, meth use rose from 3 to 4 percent of the overall population. SAMHSA statistics reveal that this is higher than the percentage of heroin users, which increased from 1 to 2 percent of the population nationwide and is considered an epidemic.[3] Fewer meth labs clearly did not translate to fewer people using meth. This is because when US meth production dropped off, Mexican gangs started bringing meth into the United States.

SHIFTING WHAT THEY INVESTIGATE

US police departments no longer direct their resources toward locating and busting big meth labs. Instead, they investigate who is working to bring Mexican meth into their communities. Jefferson County, which is located in eastern Missouri, has a unit focused on long-term investigations into suppliers in places such as Kansas City and Springfield, Missouri, and Chicago, Illinois.

PURE AND CHEAP

The meth made in Mexico is very pure. In Mexico, meth

is known as *hielo*, or "ice" in Spanish. And its purity makes it incredibly potent.

The influx of meth from Mexico has created an abundance of cheap meth. As a result, more people are using and becoming addicted to the drug. Experts know this because the number of people seeking treatment has grown. In 2005, 6,700 meth users in Minnesota were admitted to various treatment centers. In 2016, that number had climbed to approximately 11,600.[4]

But not everyone who uses meth lives long enough to seek help. In addition to the rise in the number of people seeking treatment, the number of people overdosing and dying from meth has gone up as well. In 2014, approximately 3,700 people in the United States died from

CROSSING THE BORDER

In 2010, US border officials seized 5,500 pounds (2,500 kg) of meth at the San Ysidro, California, crossing. In 2014, they seized 12,800 pounds (5,800 kg).[5] Estimating that a single hit, or dose, of meth is approximately 0.009 ounces (255 mg), the meth seized in 2014 represents 5.8 million hits. San Ysidro is the busiest border crossing between Mexico and the United States. Sidney Aki, the director of US Customs and Border Protection at the San Ysidro port of entry, said his staff has found meth hidden virtually everywhere in a car, including dissolved in the gas tank. One woman who tried to enter on foot wore a bra shaped out of meth. Smugglers use new technology, too. In August 2017, US Border Patrol agents saw a drone fly across the border. They tracked it to a spot approximately 2,000 yards (1,800 m) inside the border and arrested American Jorge Edwin Rivera as he removed 13 pounds (6 kg) of meth from the drone.[6] It had been flown into a residential neighborhood. Drones can fly at night, landing at a specific location. They are likely to be used in areas on either side of the border where communities are nearby.

In 2012, a soldier guarded barrels after a seizure of several tons of pure meth at a small ranch on the outskirts of Guadalajara, Mexico. Mexican drug cartels are nullifying US efforts to curb meth production.

meth overdose. In 2015, this number was 4,900. In a single year, the number of deaths from meth overdose had increased more than 30 percent.[7]

According to Judy Chase of the Heartland Center for Behavioral Change in Kansas City, Missouri, many people who use drugs think a purer drug is safer than one that is less pure. They believe a purer drug is less likely to harm them if they use it. When they start to notice physical problems related to the drug,

these users do not seek help because they do not think these symptoms can be related to taking a purer drug. Because of this delay in seeking medical attention and the continued use of the drug, their bodies often sustain more damage by the time these users finally do see medical professionals.

Johnathan Lucas, chief coroner in San Diego County, California, said that in 2016 his office saw meth-related deaths almost every day. "The last couple of years have actually been records for us," Lucas explained. "We've seen more methamphetamine-related deaths in the last couple of years than we've ever seen in the last 20 years."[8]

One reason more people are seeking treatment and more people are dying is that meth is affecting people in new geographic areas. "What we're seeing is that the use of methamphetamines has recently moved out of trailer parks and rural areas and into inner cities," said Ken Roy, medical director at Addiction Recovery Resources, a major treatment facility in New Orleans, Louisiana. "We're seeing a lot of heroin addicts [who] also use methamphetamines. It used to be the only way

US officials seized Mexican meth in Saint Louis, Missouri, fighting the work of Mexican cartels in the United States that has offset the gains made by cutting down on US-made meth.

we got meth patients was when they came to the hospital from rural areas," Roy said.[9]

POTENTIAL FOR VIOLENCE

Use of Mexican meth in dense urban areas worries law enforcement because it means the Mexican cartels are in the area, and these groups are known for being ruthless and violent in their home country. News stories about the violence in Mexico abound. Drugs are a big business, and the drug cartels that profit from selling meth do not let anyone stand in their way. Politicians, police officers, the families of these officials, and other innocent bystanders can easily become victims. In January 2014, Public Radio International reported that drug cartels in Mexico had killed 80,000 people there since 2006.[10]

So far, the worst of the violence has not come north of the border with the meth and other drugs, but that could be changing. In April 2014, three enforcers for the Sinaloa drug cartel

CARTEL VIOLENCE

Drug cartels in Mexico commit acts of violence every day, letting politicians, police officers, and citizens know not to interfere in their business. In some Mexican cities, seeing a dead body lying in a street is not unusual. In other areas, cartels execute people publicly and leave bodies hanging from bridges. Sometimes, cartels mutilate people with power saws.

From January through June 2017, authorities in Mexico investigated 12,155 homicides.[11] They found that when the military backs up police officers going to make arrests, gun fights ensue, leaving both cartel members and innocent bystanders dead.

flew from Los Angeles, California, to Saint Paul, Minnesota. They were not members of the actual Mexican cartel. They were members of MS-13, an American gang. The Sinaloa cartel had hired the MS-13 gang members to find out who had taken 30 pounds (14 kg) of meth that had gone missing.[12]

When they arrived in Saint Paul, the gang members questioned the man who had been in charge of the drug house where the meth had been kept. He blamed a local teenager. When the gang found the 19-year-old, whom they wanted to question, they kidnapped him and his friend, a local 16-year-old. The gang members told the teens they had two options: the pair could return the meth or give the gang $300,000 to repay the cartel. If the two teens failed to do one of these two things, they and their families would be killed. The gang members tied the teens to chairs, beat them, and held guns to their heads. Finally, the gang members held the 16-year-old down and began to cut off one of his fingers. Eventually, the kidnappers released the teenagers. The pair went to the Federal Bureau of Investigation (FBI) for help. The FBI captured and arrested one of the kidnappers, who pleaded guilty to the crime.

Cartel-related violence has not been limited to Saint Paul. In 2016, Saint Louis, Missouri, had 60 murders per year for every 100,000 residents.[14] Saint Louis Police Chief Samuel Dotson blamed Mexican drugs and Mexican drug cartels, although he said the drug of choice in Saint Louis is heroin, not meth. Typically, homicides spike wherever two or more cartels compete for customers. According to the DEA, as of February 2016, four cartels were operating in Saint Louis.[15] The cartels themselves are not in the city, but the gangs that represent them are, and as they compete for customers, people die. The cartels sell multiple drugs, including heroin and meth. Because of this, a boom in one drug can give rise to a boom in another.

In addition to selling meth in the United States, Mexican gangs are also selling meth in Nigeria and Malaysia.

SHAKE 'N BAKE

A boom in drug use can also lead to a new way to make the drug. In the 1980s, when ephedrine became hard to get in large enough quantities to make meth, a new formula was developed using pseudoephedrine. In the 2010s, with pseudoephedrine hard to get in bulk, and with large-scale meth manufacturing moving to Mexico, another formula has emerged.

Shake 'n bake is a small-batch method that does not require a laboratory or an open flame. Instead, makers crush pills and put them in a bottle with other ingredients. Next, they shake the bottle to cause the chemical reaction. This is how the meth at the

Cove hotel in Lake Geneva was being made. Often, this meth is made for a local dealer by someone who wants to trade the meth for heroin.

This new method of making meth can be done in the city as well as in the country. This is because it does not require anhydrous ammonia. Ammonium nitrate has replaced that component. Ammonium nitrate is found in the instant cold packs available at many stores.

Making meth in a bottle may differ in several ways from making it in bulk in a lab, but one thing is still the same. As the situation at the Cove showed, this new method is just as highly volatile. A small amount of oxygen in the bottle is likely to lead to a fireball. Unscrewing the bottle cap too fast can also result in an explosion. Shake the mixture in the wrong way, and the pressure builds up too fast, causing the bottle to rupture. Authorities in Alabama, Oklahoma, and other states have attributed flash fires to this method of making meth. And some of the fires have been deadly.

In the old labs, people could often escape a fire by running from the back room or garage in which they were working. With this new method, the drug can be made just about anywhere. Cooks have made meth sitting on a couch, in a bathroom stall, and while driving. The problem is that someone is likely to be holding the mixing bottle when it explodes. "When these things

THE LINK BETWEEN METH AND HEROIN

Heroin is a much more expensive drug than meth. People who can no longer afford to buy the heroin they want often steal to support their habit, but this puts them at risk for jail time, so their dealers often suggest something else. "They're now being taught by individuals to cook methamphetamine," said Captain Robert Hall of the Walworth County Drug Unit in Wisconsin.[17] An individual can still buy enough pseudoephedrine to make a small batch of meth. They do so, give it to the dealer, and get their heroin in return.

pop, you see more extreme burns because they are holding it. There are more fires and more burns because of the close proximity," said Mark Woodward, spokesperson for the Oklahoma Bureau of Narcotics and Dangerous Drug Control.[16] And the fact that the person making the drug may be on meth or in need of a heroin fix does not help the situation. Cooking meth involves dangerous, potentially explosive chemical reactions, and the people making it may be mentally and physically impaired due to their own drug use.

FINDING MORE EFFECTIVE TREATMENTS

Making it harder to get the essential ingredients to make meth did not get rid of meth in the United States. It simply shifted the problem from one of large-scale labs brimming with toxic waste to new suppliers and a new recipe. And with these have come gang violence on behalf of the cartels and more meth addicts. The Mexican cartels were able to come in to supply meth because people want the drug.

Many scientists and health-care professionals think the key to reducing the number of meth addictions is finding new ways to help people stop using meth and stay off the powerful drug. These experts believe that if they can reduce the market for meth, they will cut the effects the drug and the cartels have on the United States.

In 2015, researchers at the University of California, Los Angeles, published the results of a study they conducted. The scientists wanted to see if naltrexone, a drug used to treat people who are addicted to alcohol, would be effective in treating people who are addicted to meth. During a four-day hospital stay, researchers gave 30 participants either naltrexone or a placebo.[18] On the last day of the hospital stay, subjects received meth to monitor how they reacted to the drug. Those who had taken naltrexone had lower heart rates, lower sex drives, and were less high. Naltrexone also reduced their craving for more meth. After ten days, the participants had another four-day hospital stay. The people who had received naltrexone during the first stay received a placebo, and those who had taken a placebo received naltrexone. The results were the same—those who had taken naltrexone were less high when given meth. This study is promising, but additional research is needed before the medication can be used in real-life situations.

Anti-meth artwork by students in Montana is posted throughout the state, part of a campaign by Montana Meth Project.

In 2017, the National Institute on Drug Abuse awarded a grant to a research team from InterveXion Therapeutics and the University of Arkansas for Medical Sciences. The team will use the three-year, $8 million grant to fund a project called Study of Antibody for Methamphetamine Outpatient Therapy, or STAMPOUT. The antibody in question binds to the meth in the person's body and keeps it from going into the brain. This prevents the person from getting high from meth. Researchers hope that if patients cannot get high on meth, they will stop

using it and stay in treatment. If approved, this therapy could be used alongside behavioral therapy to treat meth addiction.

Medical professionals working with scientists continue to seek a deeper understanding of drug use and addiction. As they come to know more, they can use this knowledge to create treatments and therapies that will be increasingly successful in helping people quit using meth and other highly addictive drugs. When the market for meth has been eliminated, doctors, advocates, and law enforcement hope the problems associated with it will be eliminated as well.

ESSENTIAL FACTS

EFFECTS ON THE BODY

- Methamphetamine, or meth, is a stimulant. Stimulants wake people up and make them feel more alert. Stimulants are also highly addictive, and people quickly build a tolerance to them, including meth. This leads to using more of the drug more often.

- Too much meth can damage a person's cardiovascular system and cause kidney failure. Meth destroys a user's teeth and leads to psychosis.

LAWS AND POLICIES

- Because meth is against the law, people who take it are at risk for fines and prison sentences. These fines and prison terms include both state and federal penalties and may include city penalties as well.

- In an attempt to curb the meth epidemic, federal lawmakers worked to regulate and limit pseudoephedrine, one of the essential ingredients in meth. President George W. Bush signed the USA Patriot Act into law in March 2006. The limitations created by this law put an end to large-scale meth labs, but Mexican drug cartels now supply meth to users in the United States.

- Statistics show there is a racial disparity when it comes to drug use and jail time. Whites tend to use most illegal drugs more than blacks, while blacks tend to go to prison for possession more often than whites.

IMPACT ON SOCIETY

- When the meth consumed in the United States was mostly cooked in meth labs, the epidemic was largely a rural problem. Although some meth is still cooked in large labs, a new form of meth that does not require a laboratory has led to a movement of the drug into cities.

- Mexican cartels have begun supplying a purer form of meth. This addition to the meth landscape in the United States has resulted in gang-related violence as various gangs work in support of the cartels they represent.

- Meth is highly addictive, and researchers are working to develop prescription drugs or other therapies to make getting off meth easier.

- The prison system has borne additional costs as people are imprisoned for meth and other drug offenses. This includes having to provide health and dental care for these prisoners.

- Employers pay a price for employing addicts who might not be productive or who might miss work altogether. These workers sometimes steal from their employers, and they might use their medical insurance more, which also costs their employers.

- Environmentally, the toxic waste from cooking meth harms the areas in which it is left.

- The human toll is the damage to relationships with friends and family. And the immediate cost to users is mental and physical suffering. For some, this includes death.

QUOTE

"What we're seeing is that the use of methamphetamines has recently moved out of trailer parks and rural areas and into inner cities."

—Ken Roy, medical director of Addiction Recovery Resources, a major treatment facility in New Orleans, Louisiana

ADDICTIVE

Causing a person to want and become physically or mentally dependent.

CARTEL

A group of people in the same business who fix prices and limit competition.

COMPONENT

A part of a larger whole, an ingredient.

CONVULSION

A sudden, strong shaking of the body; a seizure.

DETOX

Time during which the body rids itself of toxins or unhealthy substances.

DISPARITY

A difference between two or more things.

HYPERTHERMIA

The condition of having a higher-than-normal body temperature, or a fever.

METH PSYCHOSIS

The combination of paranoia and aggression that results from extensive meth use.

NARCOTIC

A drug that affects a person's brain and is often dangerous and against the law to have, sell, or use.

PARAPHERNALIA

Items for a specific activity, such as to use drugs.

PARKINSON'S DISEASE

A condition in the brain that causes a person to tremble, move slowly, struggle with balance, and walk with a shuffle.

PLACEBO

A harmless substance that is given like a medicine to someone but that has no physical effect.

PSYCHOSIS

A period of mental and emotional impairment during which a person loses touch with reality, causing him or her to act strangely and believe things that are not true.

REHAB

A program designed to help people stop using addictive substances.

RHABDOMYOLYSIS

A breakdown of muscle tissue as a result of fever and convulsive twitching that can release toxins and lead to kidney failure.

SCHIZOPHRENIA

A mental illness in which a person has a distorted view and understanding of the world that interferes with his or her ability to function normally; the person thinks, feels, and behaves abnormally.

TOXIN

A poison.

WITHDRAWAL

The act of stopping use of a drug; the physical and mental side effects that occur when someone stops using a drug.

SELECTED BIBLIOGRAPHY

"Meth Addiction and the Effects in Teens." *DrugRehab.us*. DrugRehab.us, n.d. Web. 18 Oct. 2017.

"Meth Damages Brains of Teens Far More Than Adults." *Promises Treatment Centers*. Promises Treatment Centers, 9 Oct. 2015. Web. 18 Oct. 2017.

Vestal, Christine. "A New Meth Surge Gathers Momentum." *Pew Charitable Trusts*. Pew Charitable Trusts, 18 May 2017. Web. 17 Oct. 2017.

Warth, Gary. "The Neuroscience of Meth—From Pleasure to Paranoia, Drug's Effects Explained through Brain Chemistry." *San Diego Union-Tribune*. San Diego Union-Tribune, 26 Aug. 2007. Web. 30 Oct. 2017.

FURTHER READINGS

Farrell, Courtney. *The Mexican Drug War*. Minneapolis: Abdo, 2012.

Iorizzo, Carrie. *Crystal Meth*. New York: Crabtree, 2012. Print.

Sheff, Nic. *Tweak: Growing Up on Methamphetamines*. New York: Atheneum Books, 2009. Print.

ONLINE RESOURCES

Booklinks
NONFICTION NETWORK
FREE! ONLINE NONFICTION RESOURCES

To learn more about meth, visit **abdobooklinks.com.** These links are routinely monitored and updated to provide the most current information available.

MORE INFORMATION

For more information on this subject, contact or visit the following organizations:

DRUG ENFORCEMENT ADMINISTRATION

8701 Morrissette Drive
Springfield, VA 22152
202-307-1000
dea.gov

This federal department enforces banned-substance policies and makes available a wide variety of news stories and general information about meth.

DRUGABUSE.COM

877-906-3714
drugabuse.com

This organization makes available information on a variety of drugs, including meth, to those who may need help. The site includes forums and assistance in helping find treatment.

PARTNERSHIP FOR DRUG-FREE KIDS

352 Park Ave. S., Ninth Floor
New York, NY 10010
212-922-1560
drugfree.org

Previously known as Partnership for a Drug-Free America, this organization supports families by providing information and assistance and has a contact form to ask specific questions.

CHAPTER 1. FIGHTING FIRE

1. Jonah Beleckis. "Badly Burned Woman from Lake Geneva Hotel Explosion Now Charged with Making Meth." *GazetteXtra*. GazetteXtra, 20 June 2017. Web. 16 Oct. 2017.

2. "The Cost of Meth Addiction." *AddictionBlog.org*. AddictionBlog.org, 2018. Web. 6 Mar. 2018.

3. "Meth Abuse and Addiction Effects, Signs, and Symptoms." *Mount Regis Center*. Mount Regis Center, 2018. Web. 4 Mar. 2018.

4. Paul Mackun and Steven Wilson. "Population Distribution and Change: 2000 to 2010." US Census Bureau. March 2011. *Census.gov*. US Census Bureau, 2018. Web. 6 Mar. 2018.

5. Christine Vestal. "A New Meth Surge Gathers Momentum." *Pew Charitable Trusts*. Pew Charitable Trusts, 18 May 2017. Web. 17 Oct. 2017.

6. "Overdose Death Rates." *National Institute of Drug Abuse*. National Institutes of Health, Sept. 2017. Web. 18 Oct. 2017.

7. Sammi Wendling. "Costs for Meth Lab Fire Approaches $100,000." *Lake Geneva Regional News*. Lake Geneva News, 12 Apr. 2017. Web. 17 Oct. 2017.

8. Wendling, "Costs for Meth Lab Fire Approaches $100,000."

9. Wendling, "Costs for Meth Lab Fire Approaches $100,000."

10. Gerard Ross and Marie C. Sternquist. "Methamphetamine Exposure and Chronic Illness in Police Officers." *Toxicology and Industrial Health*. National Center for Biotechnology Information, US National Library of Medicine, Sept. 2012. Web. 17 Oct. 2017.

11. Brian Rokos. "Drug Houses Pose Danger to Neighbors, Homebuyers, Police; Here's How to Spot Them." *Press-Enterprise*. NP, 8 Oct. 2017. Web. 16 Oct. 2017.

12. Rokos, "Drug Houses Pose Danger."

CHAPTER 2. ABOUT METH

1. Christopher Hobbs. "Ma Huang: Appropriate vs. High-Risk Uses." *Christopher Hobbs*. Christopher Hobbs, 1998. Web. 6 Mar. 2018.

2. "Effects of Meth on a Community." *WSFA.com*. Raycom Media, 2018. Web. 6 Mar. 2018.

3. "New 'Shake-and-Bake' Method for Making Crystal Meth Gets around Drug Laws." *NY Daily News*. NYDailyNews.com, 25 Aug. 2009. Web. 16 Oct. 2017.

4. "What Is Meth Made From?" *Foundation for a Drug-Free World*. Foundation for a Drug-Free World, 2018. Web. 6 Mar. 2017.

5. "Database Tracks Purchase of Meth Ingredients." *Crystalmethaddiction.org*. Crystalmethaddiction.org, 2018. Web. 6 Mar. 2018.

6. John Barnes and Jim Lynch. "Meth Trash Piling Up Across Michigan." *Detroit News*. Detroit News, 10 June 2015. Web. 25 Apr. 2018.

CHAPTER 3. METH AND THE BRAIN

1. "How Meth Destroys the Body." *PBS Frontline*. WGBH, 17 May 2011. Web. 16 Oct. 2017.

2. "The Stages of the Meth 'Experience.'" *Foundation for a Drug-Free World*. Foundation for a Drug-Free World, 2018. Web. 6 Mar. 2018.

3. "Frequently Asked Questions." *PBS Frontline*. WGBH, 17 May 2011. Web. 16 Oct. 2017.

4. "Meth Damages Brains of Teens Far More Than Adults." *Promises Treatment Centers*. Promises Treatment Centers, 9 Oct. 2015. Web. 18 Oct. 2017.

5. Jordan M. Buck and Jessica A. Siegel. "The Effects of Adolescent Methamphetamine Exposure." *Frontiers in Neuroscience*. National Institutes of Health, Apr. 2015. Web. 18 Oct. 2017.

CHAPTER 4. OTHER PHYSICAL EFFECTS

1. "The Stages of the Meth 'Experience.'" *Foundation for a Drug-Free World*. Foundation for a Drug-Free World, 2018. Web. 6 Mar. 2018.

2. Kate Lyons. "How Young Women Desperate to Be Slim Are Using Crystal Meth to Control Their Weight." *Daily Mail Online*. Associated Newspapers, 27 Feb. 2014. Web. 31 Oct. 2017.

3. Lyons, "How Young Women Desperate to Be Slim Are Using Crystal Meth."

4. Sekon Won, et al. "Methamphetamine-Associated Cardiomyopathy." *Clinical Cardiology*. 27 Aug. 2013. National Center for Biotechnology Information, US National Library of Medicine, National Institutes of Health, 2018. Web. 6 Mar. 2018.

5. "A Note from Rehabs.com about Addiction and Stigma." *Rehabs.com*. Rehabs.com, 2018. 6 Mar. 2018.

6. "Stimulant Abuse and Hyperthermia." *Promises Treatment Centers*. Promises Treatment Centers, 12 Feb. 2013. Web. 6 Mar. 2018.

CHAPTER 5. PERSONAL EFFECTS

1. "Methamphetamine." *National Institute on Drug Abuse*. National Institutes of Health, Feb. 2017. Web. 6 Mar. 2018.

2. "The Stages of the Meth 'Experience.'" *Foundation for a Drug-Free World*. Foundation for a Drug-Free World, 2018. Web. 6 Mar. 2018.

3. "How Meth Destroys the Body." *PBS Frontline*. WGBH, 17 May 2011. Web. 16 Oct. 2017.

4. "Meth Come-Down Guide and Tips." *AddictionResource*. AddictionResource.com, 2018. Web. 6 Mar. 2018.

5. "Meth Come-Down Guide and Tips."

6. Kate Storey. "I Was a Vice Cop . . . and a Meth Addict." *New York Post*. NYP Holdings, 9 Apr. 2014. Web. 15 Dec. 2017.

7. Storey, "I Was a Vice Cop."

8. Storey, "I Was a Vice Cop."

9. Storey, "I Was a Vice Cop."

10. Bob Sullivan. "The Meth Connection to Identity Theft." *NBC News*. NBCNews.com. 10 Mar. 2004. Web. 15 Dec. 2017.

11. Sullivan, "The Meth Connection."

12. Storey, "I Was a Vice Cop."

13. "'Ultimate Party Drug' Starts Downhill Skid." *National Meth Center*. National Meth Center, 2008. Web. 4 Mar. 2018.

14. Gary Herron. "Statistics Tie Meth to as Much as 70 Percent of Property Crimes." *RRObserver.com*. Rio Rancho Observer, 26 Dec. 2012. Web. 16 Dec. 2017.

CHAPTER 6. QUITTING METH

1. "Stage 1: Withdrawal." *Quitting Crystal Meth*. NP, n.d. Web. 6 Mar. 2018.
2. "People Fergie." *AP Images*. Associated Press, 31 Aug. 2016. Web. 4 Mar. 2018.
3. "Meth Overdose: How Much Amount of Meth to Overdose?" *Addictionblog.org*. AddictionBlog.org, 8 Apr. 2014. Web. 1 Nov. 2017.
4. "How Much Does Rehab Cost?" *Recovery Village*. Recovery Village, n.d. Web. 14 Dec. 2017.
5. "The Stages of the Meth 'Experience.'" *Foundation for a Drug-Free World*. Foundation for a Drug-Free World, 2018. Web. 6 Mar. 2018.

CHAPTER 7. LEGAL CONSEQUENCES

1. Saki Knafo. "When It Comes to Illegal Drug Use, White America Does the Crime, Black America Gets the Time." *HuffPost*. 18 Sept. 2013. Web. 2 Jan. 2018.
2. "Federal Trafficking Penalties." *Illinois Eastern Community Colleges*. IECC, n.d. Web. 2 Nov. 2017.
3. "Federal Trafficking Penalties."
4. "Methamphetamine Sale, Manufacturing, Possession." *O'Meara Law LLC*. O'Meara Law LLC, n.d. Web. 18 Oct. 2017.
5. Kelly Vyzral. "Updated Federal and State Methamphetamine Law Summary." *Ohio Pharmacists Association*. Ohio Pharmacists Association, 2018. Web. 16 Oct. 2017.
6. Vyzral, "Updated Federal and State Methamphetamine Law Summary."
7. "Pseudoephedrine: Legal Efforts to Make It a Prescription-Only Drug." *Public Health Law/CDC*. Centers for Disease Control and Prevention, n.d. Web. 2 Nov. 2017.
8. Allison Gilchrist. "Patients Strongly Oppose Prescription-Only Pseudoephedrine." *Pharmacy Times*. Pharmacy & Healthcare Communications, 16 Aug. 2015. Web. 2 Nov. 2017.
9. "Prescription-Only Pseudoephedrine Approach Working, GAO Reports." *Occupational Health and Safety*. 1105 Media, 14 Feb. 2013. Web. 2 Nov. 2017.
10. "How Meth Destroys the Body." *PBS Frontline*. WGBH, 17 May 2011. Web. 16 Oct. 2017.
11. "The Costs of Methamphetamine Use: A National Estimate." *Rand Corporation*. Rand Corporation, 2009. Web. 2 Nov. 2017.
12. "Prisons and Drugs." *Drug War Facts*. NP, 2018. Web. 6 Mar. 2017.

CHAPTER 8. THE CURRENT SITUATION

1. Christine Vestal. "Meth Making a Comeback but It's Not Your Neighbors Cooking It Anymore." *St. Louis Post-Dispatch*. Lee Enterprises, 17 July 2017. Web. 16 Oct. 2017.
2. Vestal, "Meth Making a Comeback."
3. Vestal, "Meth Making a Comeback."
4. Christine Vestal. "A New Meth Surge Gathers Momentum." *Pew Charitable Trusts*. Pew Charitable Trusts, 18 May 2017. Web. 17 Oct. 2017.
5. Kenny Goldberg. "San Diego: Addicted to Meth." *KPBS*. KPBS Public Broadcasting, 27 June 2016. Web. 3 Nov. 2017.
6. Stephen Dinan. "Drones Become Latest Tool Drug Cartels Use to Smuggle Drugs into the US." *Washington Times*. Washington Times, 30 Aug. 2017. Web. 3 Nov. 2017.

7. Vestal, "A New Meth Surge."

8. Goldberg, "San Diego: Addicted to Meth."

9. Vestal, "A New Meth Surge."

10. "Mexico Drug War Fast Facts." *CNN*. Cable News Network, Turner Broadcasting System, 20 Feb. 2018. Web. 6 Mar. 2018.

11. Kate Linthicum. "Mexico's Bloody Drug War Is Killing More People Than Ever." *Los Angeles Times*. Los Angeles Times, 22 July 2017. Web. 6 Mar. 2018.

12. Paul McEnroe. "Police: Mexican Drug Cartel Enforcers Torture Two Teenagers in St. Paul." *Star Tribune*. Star Tribune, 6 May 2014. Web. 3 Nov. 2017.

13. Rick Bella. "New Drug Report: Meth Still Oregon's No. 1 Problem, Run Mostly by Mexican Drug Traffickers." *Oregonlive: The Oregonian*. Oregon Live, 21 June 2015. Web. 18 Oct. 2017.

14. Sean Kennedy. "American Carnage Is Real, Concentrated in City Pockets and Fueled by Mexican Cartels." *Real Clear Investigations*. RealClearInvestigations.com, 30 Jan. 2017. Web. 3 Nov. 2017.

15. Kennedy, "American Carnage is Real."

16. "New 'Shake-and-Bake' Method for Making Crystal Meth Gets around Drug Laws." *NY Daily News*. NYDailyNews.com, 25 Aug. 2009. Web. 16 Oct. 2017.

17. Jonah Beleckis. "Meth and Heroin in Walworth County: Two Epidemics Linked." *GazetteXtra*. GazetteXtra, 25 June 2017. Web. 6 Mar. 2018.

18. "Potentially Effective Treatment for Methamphetamine Addiction Identified." *ScienceDaily*. ScienceDaily, 19 May 2015. Web. 3 Nov. 2017.

INDEX

addiction, 18, 55–57, 59–60, 67–68, 69, 70, 81, 83, 97, 99
Aki, Sidney, 87
Alliance Environmental Group, 13
American Detoxification Project, 12
amphetamines, 16, 17, 18

Bettger, Athena, 81
binging, 38, 41, 48, 52
brain damage, 29, 31
Bush, George W., 76

cardiotoxicity, 39
cardiovascular health, risks to, 38–41
cartel, 91–93, 96–97
cartel violence, 91–93
Centers for Disease Control and Prevention, 9
Chase, Judy, 87
children, 12, 13, 24, 59
cocaine, 6, 9, 18, 29, 38
Combat Methamphetamine Act, 76–77
Cove of Lake Geneva, 4, 6, 7, 9, 11, 12, 95

dialysis, 42
dopamine, 26, 28, 29, 31–32, 64–65
Drug Enforcement Administration (DEA), 72, 74, 78, 93

ephedra, 16
ephedrine, 16, 18, 19, 93
epidemic
   heroin, 86
   meth, 8–9, 76, 83

fever, 41, 54

gangs, 86, 92, 93, 96

halitosis, 48
hallucinations, 31, 32–34, 43, 53, 54
Heringlake, Chris, 81
heroin, 9, 13, 18, 67, 74, 86, 90, 93, 95, 96
"Horrors of Methamphetamines, The," 43
hyperthermia, 43–46

InterveXion, 98

Jefferson County, Missouri, 84, 86

kidney failure, 20, 41–42
Kuen, Melissa, 6–7, 9

law enforcement, 10, 23, 53, 76, 81, 91, 92, 99
legal penalties, 71, 72, 75–76
Lucas, Johnathan, 89–90
lying, 56

Massey, Steven, 57
McBean, Patrick, 7, 9
meth
   and the brain, 18, 24, 26, 29, 31–35, 40, 46, 59, 98
   components, 19, 20–21
   cooking, 10, 18–20, 22–24, 61, 95, 96
   death, 9, 40, 64, 89–90
   forms, 8, 14, 17, 19, 52
   ingredients, 6, 12, 16, 19, 24, 47, 57, 93, 96
   labs, 18, 22, 23, 61, 80–81, 84, 86, 93, 95, 96
   nicknames, 6
   pure, 14, 75, 86–87, 88–89
   recovery, 9, 64, 65, 70–71
   waste, 7, 12, 23, 24, 96
meth mouth, 46–48, 81
meth psychosis, 33, 53

Mexico, 81, 83, 86–87, 91, 93
Moore, Allison, 55–57, 58, 61
MS-13, 92
muscle failure, 41–42

Nagayoshi, Nagai, 16
naltrexone, 97
National Center for Health Statistics
   (NCHS), 9
needles, 24, 58, 59
Novotny, Dan, 6–7

obsessive behavior, 28, 52
officer risk, 10, 12
Ogata, Akira, 17
overdosing, 9, 10, 43, 46, 64, 65, 87–88

paranoia, 31, 32, 33
Parkinson's disease, 29, 31
parole, 75, 83
Phillips, Kevin, 10
prison, 8, 74, 75–76, 81, 83
pseudoephedrine, 18, 19, 20, 22, 76–78,
   80–81, 83, 84, 93, 96
   prescription, 78–79
   regulation of, 78

race, 74
Rawson, Richard, 28
relationships, 59
Rivera, Jorge Edwin, 87
Roy, Ken, 90–91
rural areas, 8, 13, 22–23, 61, 90–91

Schwalbenberg, Dick, 12
sex, 28, 58–59
shake 'n bake, 93–95
skin damage, 10, 22, 59, 42–43
state penalties, 76
stealing, 57–58, 60
stimulant, 6, 8, 16–18, 36, 38, 64
Substance Abuse and Mental Health
   Services Administration (SAMHSA),
   86

treatment, 42, 57, 61, 67, 69–71, 80, 87, 90,
   96, 99
triggers, 70
tweaking, 52, 53–55

Volkow, Nora, 31

weight loss, 36, 38
Williams, Steve, 57
Woodward, Mark, 23, 96

Sue Bradford Edwards is a nonfiction author who writes about health and science, history, and race. She has written 12 books for Abdo Publishing, including *The Dakota Access Pipeline*, *The Zika Virus*, *Women in Science*, and *Hidden Human Computers*. She lives in Missouri.